Mindy
Farmer's Daughter, Farmer's Wife

by Mildred Gaasland

Cover design and illustrations by author

Mildred Gaasland

Published in 1994
by
Pekin Publications
523 Second Avenue N.E.
Glenwood, MN 56334-1407

ISBN 0-9639777-1-7

Mindy
Farmer's Daughter, Farmer's Wife

First printing, January, 1994
Second printing, May, 1994
Third printing, January, 1995

Printed in the USA
by

Echo Printing

Alexandria, MN 56308

ISBN No. 0-9639777-1-7 9.95

Dedication

To Karen, my daughter,
who
taught me a thing or two
about writing

Author's Note to Reader

Many of these narratives about life in the Great Depression were originally written for a local publication. Each was a separate story, and the result of this compilation is a small amount of repetition.

Mindy

Table of Contents

Working with Whitefaces

The cattle chute was in place outside the open barn door to the south, and our 73 beef stock cows with their calves were penned outside the north door, ready to be sent through a maze of pens and alleyways in the barn. One animal at a time would find its way to the cattle chute. The chute was a prison built of two-inch pipes, and it had the width and length to take a big cow. At the rear was a drop gate, and in front was a push-out gate, requiring two people to operate the chute efficiently. The front gate would close around the animal's neck, holding her securely.

John and I had no son or hired hand on our farm, so I felt it was my duty to help him treat the cattle for pinkeye. This was the only actual farm work that I did on a regular basis. Pinkeye had attacked with a vengeance that summer of 1975, so I was needed to help with this job more than once.

Herefords seem to be especially susceptible to pinkeye because of their white faces and pigmentless eyelids. The eyes get runny as the flies persist in biting the vulnerable area around them. Dust, pollen and bright sun irritates the sore eyes, causing both the eyeballs and the eyelids to become red and infected. The eyeball can ulcerate, forming a large white bump that can break open and drain. If untreated it will cause blindness.

Our most effective treatment was to squirt prepared medication into the eye with a squirt bottle. If the problem was especially bad, we glued an eye patch over the eye to keep out irritants. We had earlier discovered we could make cheaper eye patches than commercial ones by cutting nine-inch circles from blue denim yardage and sewing a pie-shaped tuck in one place from the center to the edge. The patch looked like a nearly-flat cone. John had sent for two fat tubes of glue, the kind sales barns use to glue numbers on an animal's hip, because it had great sticking power. I would squeeze out a line of glue around the inside edge of the patch, place the patch over the infected eye, and press it down.

I had worked about three hours preparing 60 eye patches, averaging about three minutes to cut and sew each one. I had smiled as I worked, remembering how elated the clerk in the dry goods store was when I bought five yards of her best quality blue denim, and how irritated she became when she learned that it was to be cut up for eye patches for cattle.

Not every animal had pinkeye, but as it turned out when we examined them, close to 70 percent of them needed treatment. Of those perhaps half needed an eye patch. A few needed patches on both eyes. They could smell water and grass and get around quite successfully thus blindfolded, and they were able to stay with the herd. Mamma cows found their calves by smell and by bellowing. Brushing up against things eventually loosened some of the patches so that some would fall off before it was time to remove them about two weeks later.

We were getting an early start that day, and we worked fast while it was relatively cool. July had already come up with some near-record scorchers with humidity to match, and this was going to be one of those days. Already the pesky flies were chewing on my ankles, and I applied some repellent.

Bonnie, our Border Collie-English Shepherd dog, helped chase a third of the herd through a bottleneck of fencing panels that forced the cattle toward the barn door. John sorted them as they entered, putting the cows into the pen nearest the chute and the calves into another pen. Separation brought on a lot of bellowing, so it became impossible to communicate with John in all that noise. Bonnie and I chased in more cattle when these were processed, and the two herd bulls would be treated last of all.

John's job was to sort, then prod with a stick and slap with a horse whip to get them into the chute. "Get in there you fat, lazy beast!" he yelled. Often the adjectives were more colorful. John loved the animals and was never cruel, but Herefords are tough beef animals and are sometimes very stubborn. Slaps and smacks with the whip did not seem to bother them much. At times John had to twist a cow's tail to get her to move. Twist it hard. John would occasionally take a kick from a spunky or fearful calf, and whenever this kind of job was done he would check his legs for serious black and blue spots. Some of these spots would last for weeks.

My job was to operate the lever slamming the front gate around the cow's neck, then to open the sore eye with my left hand while squirting in the medication with my right hand. I also determined which ones needed patches and put them on.

One cannot simply request a 1200 pound Hereford cow to hold her head still and open her eyes. She would usually pull back hard on the chute gate where her big ears pinned her in place, making my job easier. But about every third or fourth animal would try the head toss, rotating her eyeballs and head as vigorously as possible with several accompanying bellows. Then I'd have to grab the nose pliers called a snubber. This blunt-ended, two-pronged grip is made to fit into a cow's nostrils, and it has a rope attached to the handles. After repeatedly chasing the nose up, down, sideways, and diagonally in a cat-and-mouse game, I usually was victorious, squeezing the handles together quickly and firmly. She was then my prisoner, and by pulling the snubber rope around a pipe and tying it, I had her head pinned where I could treat her eye. The next complication was that the other eye was on the other side of the head. I had to loosen the rope and pull the stubborn head in the opposite direction and tie it down again.

Now and then John would have to climb out of the pens to come to assist me. It was a long, sweaty job. After three hours of this, then a quick break for a sandwich, and three hours more, we still had a few calves and the herd bulls left to process.

I suddenly remembered my mother as a woman about my age, working on the farm where I grew up. As long as there was unfinished work to do, she had been there helping my father. Her main farm job had been to carry feed and water in tall five-gallon cans to the turkeys. She had days that thoroughly exhausted her just as this day was exhausting me. I felt a surge of empathy and closeness with her. My parents had farmed and struggled during the Great Depression to eke out a living, but John and I were doing this by choice, not out of real necessity. My husband and I had both been teachers and had retired to this farm in 1973 because we wanted to live on a farm.

My mother was opposed to the idea of selling our new home in Wahpeton to move to this farm, no matter that we were building a nicer house here. Our move was causing her to relive her own days of painful struggle and hard work, just pondering it, and she wanted something better for her "baby" daughter. She said little about it, but in her last letter, written shortly before we moved to our farm, she had written what she dared not speak: "John will soon tire of wading around in all that cow manure."

At the precise moment I was thinking about those words, a calf entered the chute and slipped and fell into the pudding-like manure some big cow had decorated the chute interior with, sending blobs of the wet, green stuff flying to the right and to the left. Chunks landed in my hair and across my chest, and smaller specks freckled my face and arms. I was already hot, sweaty and miserable, and my back ached in electric surges of pain. But the irony of it made me laugh aloud. Tension flowed out from me, and I couldn't stop laughing.

John appeared in the doorway, having heard my laughter. Seeing what I looked like, he could only ask, "What in the world is so funny?"

I struggled to get my laughter under control to say, "I was thinking of Mother's letter; it's not YOU wading in cow manure, it's ME!"

John grinned broadly and broke into a voiceless chuckle. "I thought you'd be in tears," he said, observing my pitiful condition. "I'll finish up. It looks like you could use a shower."

I left for the house, gratefully.

After showering and washing my hair, I watched John a moment from the kitchen window, treating one of the two big bulls. The horned head was too large to pass through the chute, so John had him tied up short to the corner post in the fence. I don't know who was more patient, John or the bull, and all went well. Our herd was known for quietness, and I think they learned this from the quiet way John usually handled them. He had to shout at them and prod them when they were stubborn, but he was never cruel to them, and the animals knew the difference.

After a quick supper I washed the dishes and we went to bed. John fell to snoring promptly. Exhausted as I was, I could not sleep. I lay awake with throbbing back and limbs, reviewing my childhood years on the farm and remembering my dear parents. John and I were working like pioneers to improve our farm just as my parents had worked on theirs. Farming methods had changed drastically from Mother's time as a farmer's wife to mine, but the values to be learned from either period remained the same. Like my mother, I was a farmer's daughter turned farmer's wife, and I decided to tell our story.

Bonnie

A Cow in the Cattle Chute

Part of the Hereford Herd on Our Farm

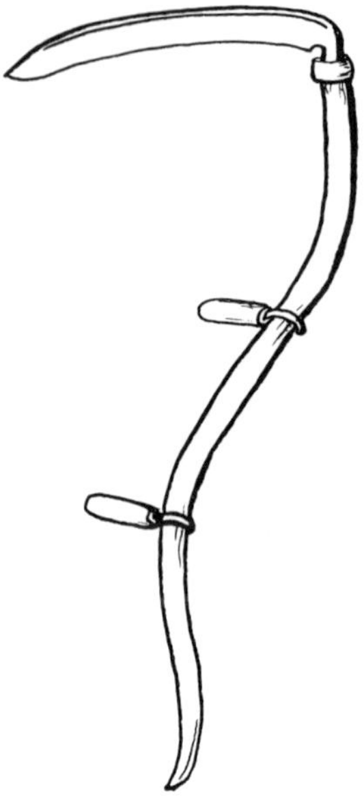

The Scythe

Cream Separator

Mindy, the Great Depression Baby

Mickey Mouse was still in infancy when I came into this world, and Herbert Hoover was our new President. I made my entry two days before spring in 1929, born on the same place where my mother and sister were born. The house still stands in use on that farm that my maternal grandparents bought when they came from Norway in 1883.

I learned to speak many words very early and to understand Norwegian as well as English, as both parents used both languages daily. But I could not say my own name, Mildred. I had just learned to walk when I started clearly referring to myself as Mindy, and I am Mindy to many people to this day. It was at least twenty years later that I discovered other individuals also had that name, much to my surprise.

My parents had, before my birth, taken a loan and purchased an eighty-acre farm on which there were only old farm buildings, but they had not yet moved there. The dilapidated house made it necessary to plan for building a new house immediately. Early in the spring, though, before we had started construction, lightning struck the old barn, burning it to the ground. A new barn had to be built first as one could not maintain milk cows without a barn, so the house would have to be on hold. My uncle, Haldor Moen, was an excellent carpenter and was available, and he came at once to begin work on a new barn.

We moved into the old house in September when I was six months old. The new Gothic-roof barn was ready by then, and construction of a six-room bungalow had already begun. We would be in the new house by Christmas.

Purchasing a new farm, having a new baby, and building two major buildings within one year was taking on a very great responsibility. No one could foresee that this was soon to be compounded by record hard times financially. The stock market collapsed on October 29, 1929. Every American was soon to be affected by the Great Depression.

As a very young child I heard my parents talk of bank failures and of persons who committed suicide because they could not handle the stress of economic losses and of Roosevelt's Bank Holiday. I did not understand these things, nor did I understand fearful talk about the "Reds" taking over our country. I was aware of my parents' fear of losing their farm, but not fully understanding the gravity of this, I did not worry about it. I did, however, sense the constant tension between my parents and experience the pain of their frequent arguments.

From my pre-school years forward I saw my parents constantly at work, usually seven full days a week. In the warm seasons there were days when I saw my father only at suppertime because he had eaten his breakfast and had gone out to work long before I was out of bed, and he worked long after the sun was down. He often took his noon meal of sandwiches with him into the field.

Father had not only the usual work to do with farm crops, haying, and tending to the milk cows, but he had to grind feed for the chickens and turkeys and to clean their pens and floors, as well as to raise a hog or two for butchering. He also had to cut down trees, to saw them into proper lengths, and to split wood for the kitchen range which was the cookstove the entire year. In cold weather it had to be kept going all day to heat water, to cook, and to heat the kitchen.

Father's work was done largely by hand and was much more physically taxing than farming is now. He had four or more work horses to stable and feed because he did not have a tractor until 1945. My parents never had electricity on their farm, and Father did not have a labor-saving milking machine, a manure carrier, or a silage unloader. He pitched silage with a fork and carried it in a big tub on his shoulder. Water came from a well and was pumped by a gasoline motor, and we were proud of our modern, individual drinking cups by each cow stanchion. In the kitchen was a small cistern pump with which we manually got soft water from the cistern in the basement. This water was rain water collected from downspouts along the roof gutters. We took our drinking water from the well and kept a pail of fresh water in the kitchen. A water dipper was shared by everyone.

One summer Father got extra work helping to build Highway 78 near Ottertail Lake. He furnished a team of horses and a wagon and his own strong arms and back. His job was to shovel black dirt with a spade onto long, foot-wide dump boards on the wagon, then to unload it in place by shoveling off some of the dirt before twisting each board sideways to set them on edge, letting the remainder of the dirt fall through. The black dirt was saved in a pile and was later put back on the shoulders of the completed highway. He put in long days and came home very tired. For his efforts he got small wages and a hernia to boot.

Mindy's Otter Tail County Farm Home

The New Red Barn, Sister Hazel

Mindy
at Two Years

Hazel Hitching a Turkey to Mindy's Wagon, Fall of 1930

Father (right) and Helper Stack Threshing, Late l920's, Flynets on Horses

Uncle Edwin Building a Grain Stack

May and John, Mindy's Parents, 1945

Mindy and Her Tame Ducklings, 1942

Mindy with Russian Blue Grandma Cat, 1946

Corn Shocks

Queen, Father's Belgian Mare, with Hazel, 1947

The long hours needed to get summer work done, coupled with the intense heat, flies, and the constant worry and hurrying often took their toll on Father's nerves. One such hot evening old Bessie refused to move up into the stanchion for milking. Father twisted her tail, slapped her flanks, and cussed and yelled, but there she stood with her hind feet stubbornly planted in the manure gutter. In this position her teats were scarcely four inches from the floor, impossible to milk.

Father kicked the cow and the cow gave him a swift kick back.

Father lost control. "Get up there, you stubborn old bitch!" he yelled as he trounced her repeatedly with his wooden milking stool.

When his rage subsided a little, the stool had a collapsed leg, and the cow's hip bone was bleeding. But the cow's head was in the stanchion. Father was almost in tears out of frustration, and, no doubt, out of a sense of shame that his young daughter had witnessed this outburst. Because I felt very sorry for the cow, I hated him in that moment. I hurriedly left the barn. Young as I was, though, I understood that the flies were mercilessly biting him as well as the cow, and that he had simply had too much pressure and trouble. This was the only time I ever saw him lose his temper and deliberately be cruel to an animal.

My mother was the only person who took daily care of my sister Hazel and me. She also had to bake cookies and cakes and to bake bread for the entire week. She kneaded the bread on the oilcloth table covering because there were no kitchen counters or cupboards. Food supplies and dishes were kept in the pantry.

Besides food preparation and keeping the house clean there were clothes to wash and ironing to do. The heavy cast iron sad irons were heated on the kitchen range. They were best handled using a pot holder when very hot.

The fire had to be kept going constantly in our kitchen range in the winter for the stove heated the kitchen as well as cooked the food. A big teakettle was always kept full of water on the back part of the stove to give us hot water at our disposal. The right side of the stove had a built-in reservoir that held five or more gallons of water. This was always warm, and we used this water to wash dishes and to wash our faces in the cold season. On rare occasions, usually right before Christmas, Mother brewed home-made root beer in the reservoir. That was a very special treat!

In addition to all these household duties, Mother managed to do many hours of heavy outdoor work as well during the warmer months. She kept a garden which had to be watered by carrying water in pails from the well. She had peonies, irises, hollyhocks, and petunias along the east wall of the house and spirea bushes to the south. Mother also carried water to chickens, turkeys, and pigs. With a scythe she cut tall weeds from around the buildings and cattle yard to keep the native grass lawn from getting weedy and also because she was a very neat person who hated weedy farmyards.

Outdoor work made it hard sometimes for Mother to make a good evening meal as she was frequently too tired, and she never had much variety of supplies to cook from. Due to either near-exhaustion or to poverty we could count on *graut* at least twice a week. This was milk, cooked and thickened to form a mush, topped with a dab of butter and some cinnamon and a teaspoon or two of sugar. My parents acted as if they enjoyed this food, but I hated *graut* when I got it too often. I could hardly swallow it. It reminded me of the thick, white school paste some kids tried eating in school. Sometimes I said I wasn't hungry and went to bed with an empty stomach to avoid eating *graut.* Then quiet tears came until I fell asleep.

Mother gathered dozens of chicken eggs laid each day in the hen house nest boxes and washed the soiled ones before packing them into thirty-dozen egg cases for market. They were traded at the Nelson Brothers Grocery in Battle Lake for groceries and cash.

In the early spring our brown Narragansett turkey hens began laying eggs. Mother took the eggs away each day, substituting them with glass eggs in the nests so each hen would continue laying in the same nest. When the hen got broody, Mother set 14 to 16 real eggs under her. The chicks hatched out, and Mother tended to them daily until they were butchered or sold for butchering late in the fall. These thirty to forty birds furnished food for us and brought in needed cash as well.

In later years my parents bought turkey chicks from the local hatchery and raised up to 500 turkeys in season. Mother carried most of the water and did much of the feeding, but Father did the heavier work.

Carrying the heavy five-gallon pails of water was how I pictured her when I, as a farmer's wife, was decorated with the manure in the cattle chute. Her work was daily, and heavy work it was.

This large number of chicks had to be kept in two brooder

houses which were built on skids, and moving the brooder houses was a family effort. To move the houses, Mother and I put round wooden fence posts in front of the skids while Father, with a team or tractor, pulled the building. As the rollers slipped out behind the house, we grabbed them and hurried to place them in front of the skids.

In summer we picked wild Juneberries and canned them into fruit sauce, and Mother made chokecherries into jelly. Lots of rhubarb was eaten in season. We canned all the garden beans, peas, and carrots we didn't eat fresh. My sister was older and of more help to Mother than I was.

After fall butchering, usually right before the Christmas season, Mother canned chunks of red meat in Mason glass quart jars and preserved side pork in salt in huge 30-gallon Red Wing crocks. All the animal fat had to be "rendered"—melted down in the oven. This liquid fat was poured over the salt pork to seal and preserve it. Hot fat was also poured over the meat in the jars just before a tight cover was put on. Fat was used in making doughnuts and in general baking and frying, too.

Mother plucked and dressed turkeys and chickens after Father had decapitated them with an axe. These she did only one or two at a time because we had no other way of preserving them than to keep them cold or frozen on our screened-in back porch.

My mother was skillful at the sewing machine. Her machine was a Minnesota pedal machine, and I now have it in my home. She never purchased a pattern to sew from because she felt she couldn't afford one. Using a garment as a pattern, she cut and sewed dresses, aprons, night gowns and pajamas for herself and for her daughters, and they usually looked great. She made nice pillowcases and bedsheets, slips and bloomers, all from bleached flour sacks. Most other women did this, too, but my mother's were much nicer. Many a pair of pillowcases and several dresser scarves were trimmed with tatted or crocheted edgings that Mother worked on during long winter evenings.

Mother used an apron daily to protect her dresses. Her aprons wore out quickly, so she sewed new ones every winter. These she made of printed cotton cloth and trimmed the edges with colorful cotton bias tape.

Heavy quilts were in constant use on everyone's beds in the '30's, and Mother made hers from leftover pieces of dress material. Mother sewed her quilt pieces by machine and tied her quilts, but I remember she went to two neighbors' quilting bees when I was perhaps eight years old. While the women sat around the quilt, stretched on the quilting frame, and stitched the quilt by hand, we children sat on the floor under the quilt and watched the sewing needles come through the fabric and get shoved back up by a silver thimble and nimble fingers. It was a very special experience for me. The work was followed by sandwiches, cake and Jello gelatin for all.

Life could have been more pleasant with a little family fun interjected into our lives on Sundays. My father, however, considered Sunday afternoons his time to rest. He preferred lying down to sleep when we three female members of the family suggested going to visit someone or going fishing or bathing in the lakes. This situation improved a little only as we girls grew older and made more forceful demands to do something interesting.

One such afternoon Mother decided to leave him at home, and she took the Model T truck with my sister and me riding in the back. We were going to visit our neighbors, the Gundersons. Enroute was an extremely steep grade down one hill followed by a steep climb up another. Just as she started down the hill she released the accelerator pedal, but it stuck in the accelerating mode, and the truck gained speed by gasoline as well as momentum. It sounded like an airplane motor reving up for take-off. Mother dared not reach down to pull the pedal back while going downhill because the dash would have obstructed her view of the road. She "let it rip," and as the truck tore down the steep grade, we heard Mother say, "*Naa kjører det som fa'en var laus!*" Translation: "Now it drives like the devil were loose!" As it tore up the next hill, it lost a little speed, allowing her to hastily dive for the pedal with her right hand and jerk it back.

As we turned into the Gunderson driveway, we saw the entire family pouring out of their house, for they had heard the terrible roar of the motor and wondered what in the world was wrong.

After that terrifying experience Mother was not so eager to strike out without her husband.

There was a lot of talk at home about not being able to afford things and talk about how poor certain families were. I hadn't been going to school long before I noticed that I was better off than many other children because I had a daily apple or orange, or at least half of one, in my lunch pail, and I always had jelly, cheese, or peanut butter on my bread. Some children had only pale oleo or pork fat on coarse white bread. My sister and I wore four-buckle overshoes when the snow came, while one or two families came to school in leather shoes with half-dollar size holes in the soles. They stuffed layers of shiny pages from the

Sears Roebuck or Montgomery Ward catalogs into their shoes to cover the holes and keep out the snow. They wore one pair of long cotton stockings while my sister and I wore two pair, plus the hated long-legged underwear when it got cold. We also had heavy snowpants. Even so, I froze a lot while walking the mile and a quarter to and from school, and my feet were cold most of the time.

Children whose parents were extremely poor qualified for Relief and had foods such as celery or grapefruit in their lunch pails. These were foods I had never seen before. My parents were never on Relief, but they did not always have the necessities and could have used help.

At one point in the mid-thirties we ran out of groceries and had no money at all. We had some potatoes left and milk from our cows, but we had run out of staples such as flour, salt, oatmeal, sugar and raisins. I knew from my parents' arguments that they were getting desperate.

Father went, reluctantly, to speak with a neighbor, and the next morning that man came to our farm, and after some haggling over price, purchased our very best Holstein milk cow for nine dollars. I can still visualize that man leading our precious cow across the field to the west. Father then hitched a team to our wagon and drove to Battle Lake with the money for supplies. Mother cried all day long. I realized much later that with that cow went our income from her cream and from her future calves. I remember that I felt very sorry for my mother as if someone had treated her cruelly. It was life under our failed economic system that had treated her cruelly, but I understood little of that.

My parents argued a lot over how various projects on the farm should be managed and over financial matters. Sometimes this turned into a real fight. But my father never struck my mother no matter how angry he became. Nor did he ever strike his children. He had a deep faith in and a fear of God which helped him in this.

One terrifying summer evening my parents continued a day-long argument until they both exploded. I was busying myself with drawing at the dining room table where our lighted kerosene lamp stood, and Father was studying the Sears Roebuck catalog as they argued. Mother was finishing work in the kitchen. They were both angry, and suddenly Father lost it. He jumped up, white in the face and frothing at the mouth as he shouted, and he threw that heavy catalog onto the floor with such force that the lamp on the table jumped.

I wouldn't have been surprised to have seen a rectangular hole through the floor. Mother came in her anger and picked up the catalog and slammed it on the table right in front of him. Father could easily have struck her, but he walked into the kitchen where he grabbed his cap and jacket and went out the door.

Father did not come in again, and half an hour, then an hour, ticked by. Mother had calmed down, and I knew she had begun to worry. She told Hazel and me to get ready for bed. We noticed that she checked the entry where he kept his gun. It wasn't there. When we were in bed, she lit the farm lantern and went out to look for him. As we peeked out the window beside our bed into the darkness, we saw the chilling sight of Mother stopping to peer into the cattle watering tank beside the barn.

Somehow we fell asleep before she returned to the house. By morning Father was back at the breakfast table. Things were back to normal. Life went on.

I could always count on my father to speak to naughty boys who were cruelly pestering my girlfriends and me while walking home from school, and the pestering would stop for a long time.

One memorable day my father lived up to my protector-image of him, and I was proud of him. An old lady whom we knew well was seen waddling toward us across the fields, and Mother, sensing trouble, went out to meet her. I followed. The old woman's face looked like chopped meat on one side. It wasn't bleeding drops of blood, but her temple and cheek were very raw and full of broken blood vessels. She staggered into our kitchen, trembling and out of breath, and sank into a chair.

Mother got her some oatmeal cookies and a glass of milk which she scarcely touched. She told us how her son had lost his temper in a discussion of family matters and had grabbed his leather razor strap in anger and whacked her a couple of times with all his strength.

My father came in then, and she told her story again. She had run out of the house to get away from him and had just kept going, and she wasn't sure she dared ever to return home again. My father, who was over six feet tall, a big-boned and very strong man, said he would take her home by car and she was not to fear. He did. He later told us of his threat to that man who was otherwise his friend. I am sure it never happened again because that man took Father's threat seriously. Families, like this one, felt great stress due to the hopelessness of the times they lived in, and it seemed to bring out the worst in everyone.

Economic struggles were compounded by extremes in weather in the '30's. There were record snowfalls and cold spells, and in summer, record droughts, dust storms, grasshopper plagues and larvae infestations, making farm profits quite impossible some years.

Sad Irons *"Sad" here has an obsolete meaning of "firm."*

Mother's daily work was finished only by going to bed at night. Father tried to relax when his evening chores were done by sitting with one ear glued to the speaker of his car battery radio. He loved to listen to the fights, and Joe Louis was his favorite boxer. Just when I had gotten to bed, I could be sure father would tune in the sports event so loud that I could hear every word with a pillow covering my head. I could not easily get to sleep having to listen to the monotonous drone of the sportscaster. I hated those nights.

On other nights there was *Fibber McGee and Molly*, a favorite of the whole family, as well as *Amos and Andy*. And *Gildersleeve*. And *The Shadow*. These were all on earlier in the evening.

On certain days after school was out and we were home again, we could listen to my favorite program, *Little Orphan Annie*. The appeal wasn't that we felt sorry for her being an orphan, but rather, the adventurous life she lived. I also enjoyed this program immensely because we could send in Ovaltine labels by mail and get secret message decoders—gold-colored, triple-layered, round pins that could decode the messages she gave us over the air. We would copy them down as she read them and decode them after the program. It made us feel like we belonged to a club.

Mother's only regular diversion was to attend monthly meetings of the Everts Birthday Club of which she was a charter member. Father's was to take in an occasional farm auction or to hunt ducks in our slough in the fall. Whenever we went to a public picnic, Father joined other men in a game of tossing horseshoes. Friends sometimes called on us on a Sunday afternoon, and only then did we listen to songs on our Edison phonograph or view 3-D scenes with our stereoscope.

Charles Lindbergh was Mother's hero. He had done the impossible by piloting his light plane solo from New York City to Paris. He was a Minnesota boy whom everyone admired. She hoped to meet him when he came to Minnesota, but this dream was not to be.

Mother also admired Amelia Earhart. She, too, captured everyone's imagination.

Some of the happier memories I have are of the P.T.A. meetings at my rural school and the Christmas program there, the school picnics at the end of the term, the annual Old Settlers Picnic in Battle Lake, the Otter Tail County Fair, Sunday School, and the times we got to go fishing or bathing in the lakes.

I also enjoyed four years in the Everts 4-H Club. As a winner of a trip to the Minnesota State Fair in 1941 at the age of 12, I was the youngest member in the 4-H dormitory those four nights.

The highlight of the fair for me was to see Sister Kenny and hear her speak. She was an Australian nurse who developed the popular hot water pack and massage treatment for paralysis caused by polio. I knew several people badly crippled by polio who had benefited from her method of treatment.

We always had cats and kittens to enjoy. And I was thrilled to raise my own flock of white Pekin ducklings for several years. The pony and the lamb I constantly dreamed of owning were just that—dreams. In winter I enjoyed skiing down the hills on the farm. There were no binders on the skis, only a strap over the arch, but I skied fairly well with what I had.

There was much that was good and fun, but the outstanding impressions that come to mind when I think of my early years in the Great Depression are those of hard work, struggle, tension, poverty, and bad weather. I believe that they all helped to make me a stronger and more content person, and so I am thankful for the down side as well as for the good times.

Disaster Strikes

I looked up from my play on our farmyard one very hot, sultry August afternoon to see a black, twisting cloud with a tail. "Look at that funny cloud," I said to Mother while I pointed to the west where there were other dark clouds around it.

Mother yelled for Father, "Come and look at this horrid cloud!"

He stuck his head out over the Dutch door of the barn with instant recognition and shouted, "Tornado! Go to the basement right now!"

We did.

Father got his eight Holstein cows into the barn where the horses already were in their stalls. Then it struck. He stayed there with the animals because he could do nothing else, but I think he must have been terrified for the safety of his wife and daughters.

I was only four years old then, but I vividly recall the terror and the noise when the wind and hail struck. I thought of long coal trains I had seen and heard, and it sounded as though one was coming through our living room above us. It was deafening, and the house creaked and shook. My sister and I huddled together with Mother who held us in her arms until all was quiet. We waited, wondering whether the storm could really be over.

We heard my father at the kitchen door, but he didn't come in. We ran upstairs to the door to see what could be wrong. He was shoveling hail away from the door in order to open it—hail piled about two feet deep! Then we saw the hail as large as goose eggs (larger than a baseball) scattered all over the yard with smaller hail among them. There were "drifts" of hail up against the buildings and bushes. Some would still be melting five days later.

Trees had lost leaves and branches and looked naked. The windows and screens on our bungalow were broken or damaged. Aside from deep chips in the siding and ruined shingles, our house and barn were intact. All seemed well enough.

Then we found our 50-some turkeys. Our turkey flock had huddled together when the wind and rain came, and they now lay mashed into the ground where they had been standing when the hail came. There was nothing to salvage.

Next we went to inspect our crops, just as our closest neighbor climbed over the boundary fence, complaining because the leaves on his corn had been badly ripped. When we got to where our cornfield came into view he stopped and exclaimed, "Oh, God!" It was not irreverence. It was an expression of disbelief at what he was seeing and of awe at the power of nature. Our six-feet tall corn had been reduced to a few 18-inch stalks left upright. Like the turkeys, it was mashed into the soil.

That evening our three adult geese came home from the slough below the barn. One hen had a broken leg, and feathers were ruffed up and broken on all. But no doubt diving into the water had spared their lives.

We had not been touched by the tornado funnel which had veered off to the northeast less than a quarter mile from us. One small corner of a wheat field escaped the path of the hail and stood unscathed.

We had our cattle, and we harvested thirteen bushels of wheat that fall. A few potatoes and carrots were in the ground, all we had to live on until the next crop. But our family was alive and well and ready to take on a new year.

Norman's Red Wagon

Norman was my blonde, pre-school playmate. His parents were poor and rented a tiny farm that seemed even poorer. People moved onto and away from that farm almost annually. Rocky, wooded and hilly, it was not a place to earn a living for a family.

The unpainted, old, two-story house gave the impression that it might have provided more space were it possible to have laid it down on its side. It was nearly hidden in the woods just a few steps from a township dirt road where our mailbox rested on a post beside theirs. The mail route that came by Norman's place was a full half-mile from my home. This is where Norman came to greet me almost daily during summer when I followed my big sister to get our mail. We stole a few moments to play with stones in the road or to pick spiderworts or black-eyed Susans in the ditches. Sometimes we peeked into the tunnel-like homes of the bank swallows in the sandy cut above the ditch.

One starry July night a terrible thing befell Norman and his parents and a hired man. They had to scramble for their lives to get out and away from their burning house. Neighbors, having seen the flames, came and found them in the yard, watching helplessly. The house had shot into flames as fast as a firecracker, Norman's father said, and he barely managed to awaken the hired man after getting his small family out. There was no chance to save anything and no telephone to call the fire department for help. Help was seven miles away, anyway.

My mother and I walked over to see the charred remains when daybreak came. Norman, in smiles, was playing outside while his parents tearfully surveyed the still-hot basement into which their meagre possessions, now useless and dead-looking, had fallen. The hired man lay asleep in his car.

Mother had brought a loaf of her home-made bread, and soon other neighbor women appeared with a jar of fruit sauce, a glass of chokecherry jelly, and some home-rolled doughnuts or whatever item of food they could spare. In these Depression years everyone had too little for themselves, and it was sacrificial to share even this much food.

Norman showed me his little red wagon, a Christmas present from a year or two ago. It was as black and ugly as the charred segments of the housewalls that stood tottering to one side, and there was no longer a hint of red paint on it. The slim, twisted rubber tires still clung to the wheels in spots as if determined not to let go. That wagon symbolized all that was good in Norman's life, and now it was totally ruined. He had no toys, no shoes, but only the worn-out denim bib overall he was wearing. He no doubt slept in them and would have to sleep in them for some time. The sight of the red wagon sickened me. I think it was the first time in my young life that I had felt sympathy for a friend, and the tears came.

It was my uncle who had come to our home that morning before dawn to tell us that Norman's house had burned to the ground. He was the closest neighbor and had been up half the night trying to help and had brought them old quilts to make sleep in their car a bit more comfortable. My uncle also told us that he was sure the fire had been set by a falling star! Others claimed to have seen a falling star over that house that night, he said.

It sounds incredible today that normally-intelligent people could have believed such a thing. Uncle Edwin, like many rural boys old enough to help out on the farm, had gone to school four or five months a year for only five years. Science was not taught, and perhaps the ill-trained teachers knew very little about astronomical proportions and activities. There was no access to a library, and while most people had a radio, the radio did not seek to educate.

Many years later my father concluded that the hired man had smoked in bed, and that may have been closer to the truth.

Norman had to move away for want of a home, and I never saw him again. But I will always remember him and his little red wagon turned black, beside the charred house basement where a star had fallen.

Remembering Our Thanks

My father was perhaps the hardiest man I have ever known. Many times over the years when we were growing up, he seemed to prove that he had the constitution of an ox and the nine lives of a cat. When it came to going to the doctor, he also had the stubbornness of a mule.

Dad cut trees for fuel every winter when he had less other farm work to do. One November day before Thanksgiving he was quite deep in the woods felling trees. There was a little snow on the ground, and it was cold. Crackling cold. He may have been getting tired, or he may have worked too hastily, and an accident happened. On one of his powerful axe swings, the axe hit a knot and glanced off the tree, slicing instead into his leather boot. The sharp blade went right into his ankle bone.

Father unlaced his boot to look at the wound, and he knew that he had to get home as fast as possible before he lost too much blood. This was during the 1930's when no one knew much about tetanus, so Father didn't think twice about taking the shortest route to our house—right through the horse manure in the cattle yard.

At first he refused to get the doctor, but when the pain got too bad, Mother ignored his protests and asked a neighbor to call for the doctor. I was only five years old at the time, so many of the events of the next several days are fuzzy in my memory. Father did get tetanus which turned into lockjaw which is deadly, even more so then when no antibiotics were available.

We had planned to start preparations for Thanksgiving Day, but now Mother had, instead, an around-the-clock vigil for her husband. She could only catnap while he slept fitfully.

I can vividly remember my father lying in bed with his wrapped ankle propped up on a pillow on top of a fifteen-dozen wooden egg case to get it elevated as much as possible. No fancy equipment. Doc Boline improvised. There Father lay on the razor's edge for many hours, just how long I can't recall. I do remember, though, that he could not open his mouth or move his limbs or respond to Mother's voice in any way for a time. I also remember how very black his skin looked.

On Thanksgiving morning the doctor came, expecting to find that we had lost the patient during the night, but there Father lay smiling weakly. He could just barely move his eyes and face muscles. No one had realized it at the time, but Father later told us that he had seen himself sometimes in the dresser mirror across the room. And there was also a time when Mother and the doctor thought he was unconscious, and the doctor had told Mother that he didn't think that my father had many hours left to live. Father had heard that.

Over the following days Father got entirely well. His normally excellent physical condition, with God's help, had brought him through. That was not to be his last flirtation with the grim reaper, though, but for that day we were unspeakably thankful that he had made it. It was by far our most thankful Thanksgiving Day.

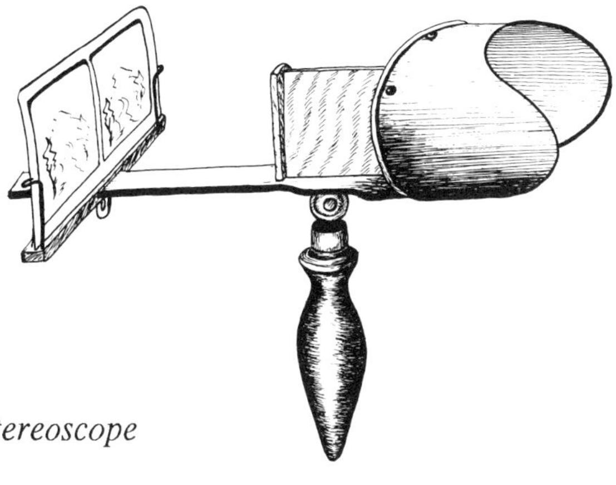

The Stereoscope

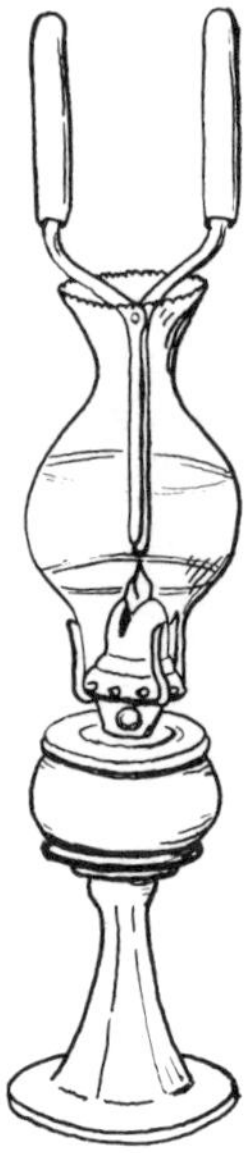

Heating the Curling Iron in the Lamp

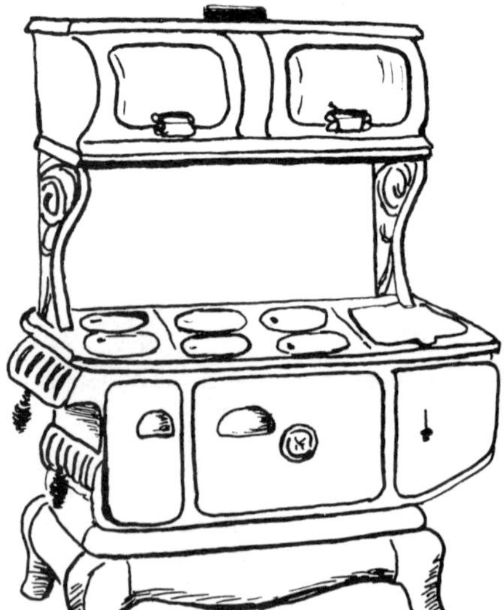

Kitchen Range

Christmas Supper Alone

The highlight of the year in the 1930's where I grew up, for both children and adults, was Christmas. It topped everything: birthdays, Thanksgiving, Easter, Halloween, and the 4th of July. It wasn't that Christmases were so very remarkable then, but nothing else was celebrated as much. The rest of the year seemed harsh and drab.

Looking back on it now, however, there doesn't seem to have been much fun at all to our Christmases when I was a little girl. The weather was usually too cold or unfriendly to do any socializing with neighbors or relatives. We kept close to our farm and the responsibility of taking care of the animals. But it was a welcome, relaxing break in the dark winter months.

Every December shortly before Christmas Mother would take us on a special treat of shopping at Woolworth's Five and Dime in Fergus Falls. It wasn't much of a treat for a small child like me, though, because at that time everything was displayed off the floor, far above a child's head. I remember being bored and feeling neglected as I clung to Mother's skirts while she walked along the high, brown, varnished counters that formed a long, dark corridor from my viewpoint. High up on the walls were mounted the dolls and larger toys not intended for fondling by grubby little hands. Even the adults had to request a sales person to get one down for closer inspection. I didn't know until I was at least nine years old what was up on those counters. Besides that, I don't recall that children under twelve years were ever permitted to buy anything.

Going into the J.C. Penny store was much more interesting. They always used a fascinating system of tubes on wires to make change. The clerk at the desk would write up a slip stating the amount of purchase and the amount tended, then subtract to indicate the amount of change. Then the bills and the slip would be attached to a clip on the outside of a five-inch long tube, and the tube was fitted into its proper place; a stong jerk of a handle attached to a cord sent it sliding posthaste up the heavy wire to the balcony where the cashier took what was needed and sent the change sliding down again in the tube. One twist and out came the change. There was such a wire going from the cashier's booth to each department in the store. This process could occupy a child's fascination for a good hour of shopping by the mother.

Our family did not attend church at Christmas as there were no services held in the vicinity of our farm, although we took in the Sunday School Christmas program in Skiptvet Lutheran Church when I began to attend at the age of eleven.

The sanctuary of that old wood-frame church was very hard to heat, and the building sat unprotected on the open prairie where the northwest wind loved to penetrate it. Parishoners who came for the Sunday School Christmas program sat in church with their winter coats and overshoes on through the evening service. During the program, some could be heard stomping their feet in an effort to keep warm, and everyone would go home with cold feet. Vapor from everyone's breath was visible in the light of the mantle lamps. If it hadn't been for the body heat generated by the room-filled crowd seated close together in the pews, the cold might have been intolerable. Even so, some people had come a half-hour early to get a good seat near the front, and as they entered, the men still went to sit on the right-hand side of the aisle and the women and children sat on the left. Nearly all had a mile or many miles to ride to get there, and while others had later model cars, some came in Model A Fords.

All the children were assigned a song or recitation to perform in front of the congregation, and I remember vividly my nervous fear of forgetting my lines as I recited the entire Parable of the Sower and the explanation of the Parable.

Following the program, a church official handed out a shiny, red apple and a brown bag of peanuts and hard candy to every child present. We also got a token gift from under the tree from our Sunday School teachers. I got a pretty celluloid book marker one year and a tiny booklet of Bible verses the next.

A warm brick kept in the oven of our kitchen range was taken out and wrapped in flannel for the foot of our bed when we got home that night. It helped warm our nearly-frozen feet.

The most unforgettable Christmas of my childhood was when I was six years old in 1935. We hadn't yet come to our special day of shopping when my sister came down with a terrible case of flu. It was only five or six days before Christmas, and Mother's only shopping had been by catalog. Nor had she finished her usual cookie and lefse baking. Now she had to care for my sister confined to the bed, and a day or two later Mother was just as sick with the flu. The next morning my father was limp and white. Only I remained well.

Mother was so ill for the next several days that Father had to tend to both of them. They had chills, body aches, and a high fever. They couldn't keep food down. Despite his own illness, Father had to go to the barn and milk our eight Holstein cows by hand, separate the cream from the milk, pump water, and feed the animals hay and silage. Silage had to be carried in heavy tubs on his shoulder from the silo outside the barn. I'll never forget how white his face was when he came in from the barn after doing his chores! He did something then that he had never done before; he stayed right in bed every hour that he wasn't helping the other sick ones or working in the barn.

Christmas Eve was coming up fast. Father dragged himself out of bed and hastily put up the Christmas tree at the foot of the two beds in the master bedroom where all four of us slept now that three were very ill. He brought out the box of decorations and went back to bed. I decorated the tree up as far as I could reach from standing on a chair. Mostly on one side. To me it looked great. Even though everyone else was in bed, I was as chipper as a chickadee and quite satisfied.

I can still visualize the dusty rolags of lint gathered on the linoleum-covered floor under the furniture. I found this quite remarkable because Mother had never before tolerated a speck of dust at Christmas. Whenever Mother shook the grates in the coal heater, she opened the little door below the pot-bellied front doors and scooped out the ashes into a pail. Ash dust settled on the lint and on the floor. Father took out the ashes and brought back a pail of coal, and poured it noisily into the hopper. I kept a finger in my ears all the while.

Mother put four boxes of Christmas gifts under the tree. There were new work stockings for Father and new slippers for her daughters and herself. These she had ordered in the mail from the Montgomery Ward catalog.

Then Mother, very weak and pale, tried to help me get my Christmas Eve supper. The others could not tolerate a bit of food, but I was as hungry as usual. She cut three or four slices off a slab of salt pork and cut up a cold, boiled potato before having to collapse into bed again. I fried this in a pan on the kitchen wood range, my first attempt at cooking. I got milk from a jar in the pantry, and I ate my Christmas supper all alone.

When Father came in from doing the evening chores, he went right to bed. I then delivered the Christmas gifts to each patient lying in bed, although they were all too ill to enjoy it then. Even so, it was Christmas Eve, and I had decorated the tree; my family was with me in the house, so I was quite content. I put my new slippers on and played under the tree with my old toys, my crayons and color book.

Coal Heater Similar to Mindy's ,
on Display at Pope County Historical Museum

Doc Boline

An April day in Minnesota can be both spring and winter in the same day. We had been experiencing balmy days, so Mother sent my sister and me to school wearing only a sweater as an outer wrap. We had a mile and a quarter to walk, but it was sunny and warm. Weather forecasting was not yet an accurate science.

By 4:00 p.m. when school was dismissed, the sky had become heavily overcast, and a cold front was angrily blowing its way through the area. Today we'd call it an Alberta Clipper. Our school group whose homes were along the road leading to the west had to walk home as no parent came to get us. The neighbors to the west of us seemed to depend upon their children catching a ride with my father as he was usually the first to fetch his children by car. But on this day he had gone to a farm auction sale many miles away. It was bone-chilling cold bucking the northwest wind, and I felt chilled all evening after we made it home on foot.

Two or three days later I was quite ill with a cold, a fever, and chest pains. Doc Boline was called from Battle Lake, and he covered the seven miles in good time. He told us that I had pneumonia in one lung. Two days after I became ill, Hazel became ill. She, we soon learned, had double pneumonia. I was then seven years, and she was ten.

Those days of illness are somewhat blurred in my memory, but certain things stand out very clearly. I had stabbing pains in my right lung, and the pain came with every breath. Mother often sat beside my bed and pressed her hand onto my side to relieve the pain until I fell asleep. We were given a white, chalky, bitter pill crushed into powder and swallowed with water. It may have been aspirin. It was a real struggle to drink it all down. Penicillin, although first discovered in 1928, and other antibiotics were not available then. We sniffed the vapor from some inhalant burned in a canister to create steam. It relieved the pain. But our own systems had to do the fighting.

Mother recorded that my temperature rose to 104 degrees, and after an unknown time it began to drop. When it did so, I hallucinated all day long. I was visited by the famous Dionne quintuplets of Canada who did a trapeeze act at the foot of my bed. Paper dolls adorned in corn silks hung at random on the bedroom walls. Ice, coated heavily on the 6-inch baseboards, began to melt. Mother thought that my crazy comments meant that I had permanently lost my mind. She nearly lost hers until Doc Boline came about 6:30 p.m. and assured her that was not the case.

When he arrived, he came first to my bed to check on my temperature which was now closer to normal. I complained to him about the fish scales that I could see covering both my forearms. He said he'd get rid of those, and he then brushed my arms vigorously with his hand. The scales disappeared like dust. Doc Boline, my friend, could cure anything, even remove fish scales from my arms! I settled back in bed peacefully while he explained to my mother that this behavior was normal after a high fever and meant only that I was recovering. I heard and understood what he said, but what I saw was no less real.

Then he turned to my sister in the other bed to take her temperature. It was at least two degrees higher than mine had been, dangerously high, he told Mother. He ordered her to find two towels and a large bowl of tepid water, quickly. Doc undressed my sister and dipped the towels into the water and wrung them out. He placed a wet towel across her thighs and used the other to wash her chest and belly repeatedly. He periodically turned her over and washed the back side. She shivered while he kept up this process for well over one hour, until her temperature came down two degrees. He had other house calls to make, so he told Mother to continue this process quite awhile longer before letting my sister go to sleep. Mother was to take her temperature often and to call him at once if it began to climb. We had no telephone, so that meant Father would have to hurry to a neighbor and call from there.

I slept most of the night with little breaks of consciousness. Whenever I was awake, I saw Mother sitting on the chair between the beds. Her two children had been too close to death's door to relax her vigil all night. But, in the morning my sister was also better. It is a wonder she escaped brain damage, Doc told us later. We certainly give him credit for preventing that!

My parents had ordered the installation of a telephone before we got sick, and after a week and a half of being in bed I lay awake in late afternoon, listening to the sounds of installation made by the telephone company employee in the kitchen. When he left, I begged Mother to see the new telephone. She helped me into a sweater and my slippers. I was so very weak that she had to hold me while I walked on wobbly legs into the kitchen where I sank into a chair. She made a quick call to my Uncle

Edwin to tell him about our new telephone. His ring was a long, a short and a long: rrrrr rrr rrrrr. Then she helped me back to my bed.

I found out what telephone rubbernecking meant in those days. When one made a call, the ring was heard in all the homes on the line, and many, if not most, lifted the receiver carefully to listen in on the conversations of others. It was not a secret because the caller could hear the "click" of each receiver as another party came on the line. Mother did this only rarely if she deemed something extremely important, but she tried to teach us that listening in on others was wrong.

As sick as my sister had been, she was back in school after two weeks. It took me four weeks to get well enough to return. I had been a light eater and suffered frequently from a runny nose and head cold which I believe now was caused by allergy. After getting sick, my body had to rally to fight off the pneumonia or else die. I guess my white corpuscles did a super job because my health improved greatly after this illness, and I got a better appetite.

For the next four winters I usually wore my leather Lindbergh aviation cap with the strap pulled tight under the chin. It kept the cold wind out of my ears.

I'll never look at an old wall telephone with a crank and mouthpiece without thinking of that very serious illness. My sister and I surely owe our lives to Doc Boline and to our vigilant mother.

Wall Telephone

Infamous 1936

The year 1936 will always be infamous in the minds of Minnesotans who can remember it. January and February were record cold that year, and a record volume of snow was dumped on our state. Summer was record hot and dry.

My maternal grandfather died on February 1, and we managed to drive the eight miles to his funeral in Underwood. My father had to shovel much of the way home because deep drifts had formed across the road that blustery day. He rammed into the drifts, penetrating some only to get stuck fast. He then shoveled snow from under the car at both ends, rocked the car to its limit, shoveled some more, then rocked the car free and soon drove into the next too-deep drift to repeat the process. My father was a tall, very strong man, but this exhausting, cold journey was about all he could take. It was below zero, and it took us well over two hours to get home.

The cities of Fargo and Moorhead recorded that, starting on January 15 and running through February 20, the temperature never got above zero! February of 1936 was the coldest month in that area in US Weather Bureau history which goes back to January 1, 1881. January at Hector Airport in Fargo had an average temperature for the month of -9.8 degrees.

**The Moorhead community in the winter of 1935-36 recorded a total of 61 inches of snow in an area that seldom gets as much as 30 inches.

My paternal grandmother died in the heat of July 24, 1936. Her funeral was preceeded by a wake, her body lying in view in her own home, and the evening was almost unbearably hot. It had been even hotter earlier. **The *Fergus Falls Daily Journal* reported that Monday, July 6th, was the hottest day ever experienced in that city when it rose to 110 degrees. The same newspaper states that the entire month of July, 1936 had an average maximum temperature of 94.5 degrees! The previous July average maximum temperature for all years was 73.7 degrees.

I can remember that the temperature reached 110 degrees in the shade for three days on our farm thermometer and remained nearly that high for three more days. My sister and mother and I spent most of those days as well as nights in our cool basement.

**Rainfall that July in Otter Tail County totaled .06 inches! In general, it was the hottest and driest July in the history of that county. I was a child of seven years and could not go barefoot because the soil burned my feet. I also hated walking anywhere outdoors because grasshoppers flew up into my face with every step. My sister and I had to help Mother weed the garden which we eventually gave up to the grasshoppers because the soil dried up and became as hard as a brick.

My family attended a Farm Bureau picnic on the southeast side of Ottertail Lake that summer. I can still relive my fear and visualize the tent caterpillars (or whatever they were) dropping from the oak tree branches overhead onto the picnic table and the bench I was sitting on, into my hair, into the Jello bowl, into the potato salad, and even onto my plate. I alternately shrieked and cried.

Farm horses dropped dead in an epidemic of sleeping sickness which was devastating because they were the farmer's power source.

People also got encephalitis. Some hired men, usually men in their prime, got sun stroke or suffered from dehydration.

Then, before we got complacent, dust storms livened things up. Tumbleweeds got caught in fencerows, and soil from western Minnesota and North Dakota built big drifts in the tumbleweeds. The sky was very dark on windy days from the blowing soil. There was a great fear of prairie fires, but I don't remember seeing one.

Threshing proved to be a game of survival that fall for those who shock-threshed (taking grain bundles right from the field versus stack-threshing.) The millions of grasshoppers had eaten nearly the entire crop in some places, a crop that was already poor from drought, and what they left behind the crickets began to devour.

It was terribly hot to work outdoors and almost as bad for the housewife who cooked for the threshing crew of about eleven hungry men. Cooking was done on the kitchen range, a wood-burning stove. The huge coffee pots had to be kept hot. This added to the heat in the kitchen and the dining room.

Threshing for me, a young child, was the most exciting farm event of the year. I covered my ears with my hands when Mr. Hanson's big gasoline tractor pulling the threshing machine rumbled by our house, causing the house to vibrate and the dishes to rattle in the cupboards. I thought the rig looked like some threatening gray monster. Mother hated the lugs on the tractor wheels because they tore up the yard.

The huge belt between the tractor and the separator both fascinated and scared me. I had heard gory stories of men being injured hooking it up. The belt had to be slipped on while the pulleys were running.

Watching the straw blow out of the pipe and the pile of golden straw growing was fun and reminded me of the story of Rumplestiltskin.

I had to help Mother carry lunch to the men at the rig both forenoon and afternoon, a lunch made up of sandwiches, cake or doughnuts, and coffee. The men took turns eating so that the threshing process did not shut down.

November 3, 1936, became an historic date in my family. We had just come through a bad snowstorm, whether of blizzard proportions or not, I can't recall. I do know that it left us with enough snow to make the use of a car unthinkable. The snow was deep everywhere and had piled into hard, deep drifts in many places.

My father was on the township governing board, and it was his duty to open the township hall for elections that day. Opening time as specified by law I believe was seven a.m., so he left in the dark with his sturdy Percherons pulling the bobsleigh.

Father was right on time when he came to a small wooded hill known locally as Rustad Hill where an abrupt little ravine had to be crossed before climbing the hill. This ravine ran into the fields on either side of the road, and as the team approached it, Father could see trouble.

The horses waded gamely into the deeper snow until they bogged down, unable to pull the bobsleigh upward through the heavy drift that loomed above them. So Father turned them to the right onto a field approach. They managed to cross this onto the field, but the big drift still hovered like an ocean wave about to burst. Father tried to take the team around the drift when they suddenly sank into snow to their bellies. Repeatedly they jumped and struggled to get free, but the bobsleigh was stuck.

Father unhitched the team from the bobsleigh, and free of their burden, they managed to jump out from the deep snow. While they stood resting, Father lifted the pole of the bobsleigh, and with his characteristic marvelous strength, he managed to turn the front portion of the sleigh to create an angle that would make pulling the sleigh easier. He backed the team into this new position, hitched them, and waded out in front of them, tugging and cajoling and slapping them with the reins until they got the sleigh free of the drift. The horses and their master retreated homeward.

Needless to say, the township hall opened very late that

election day. After Father put the horses into the barn, he went on skis to the township hall. No matter. No one came to vote until nearly noon, anyhow.

I'm glad now that I had these experiences, the bad with the good, because they helped me cope with life's difficulties later on. I have worried through the more recent droughts of 1976, 1988 and 1989, and I fear for other such years. 1936 began with a tremendous snow melt, but the intense heat wasted the moisture. I hope I never have to experience such a year as 1936 again!

**Credits to the *Fergus Falls Daily Journal* as read in the Otter Tail County Historical Society Museum, Fergus Falls, MN.

The Bobsleigh

The Saturday Night Bath

We had no electricity in our home until the year I was graduated from high school, so the Saturday night bath was something of an ordeal during the three or four coldest months. My mother had to heat bath water in huge kettles on our kitchen wood range. Mother brought up a 15-gallon, round, galvanized tub from the basement storage and set it in the center of our kitchen floor. She pumped some cold, soft rain water from the cistern and put it into the tub. Then she poured in hot water from the kettle on the stove until it felt comfortable.

I was the youngest, so I got my bath first. There wasn't as much of me to dirty the water.

When I got into the tub I could sit down with my knees pulled upward, but the others had to hunker down and use a wash cloth to help soak their upper bodies. We always had store-bought soap bars, a luxury for many farm families. It was toasty warm beside the kitchen range with a red hot fire burning in the fire compartment. The dim light of a kerosene wall lamp made it all seem cozy.

My sister bathed after me in the same water; then my mother took her bath. She added more hot water for herself. By the time my father was to bathe, we girls had been whisked out of the room off to bed. I don't really know, but I'm quite sure he got the same water—with fresh hot water added.

Father had to carry out dirty bath water after all four of us had taken a bath, and Mother cleaned the tub. Bathing meant changing clothing, so on Mondays Mother always had a big wash of towels and clothing to do in her Maytag wringer washer with the gasoline motor.

The truth is during periods of extremely cold weather we did not get a bath every Saturday night. Some families, judging by the very dirty necks of their children, did not bathe all winter!

Summer baths were taken in the same tub in our cool basement. Here the dirty water was poured into the floor drain, making the whole process much easier. If there was a drought at the time, however, the water had to be carried out and poured on the flowers or the garden.

Shampoos were easier to do. We used a water basin in the kitchen sink beside the cistern pump, but to get the proper temperature, the water had to be premixed in a large container. At least at the sink water could be released into the sink drain where it ended in a large pail.

It felt good to get clean, but Saturday night baths still were not an event I looked forward to. Nor did I like to have my face washed as a small child. Mother once came to me with a wet, soapy wash cloth and started to rub dirty areas on my face, so I asked, "Are we getting company?"

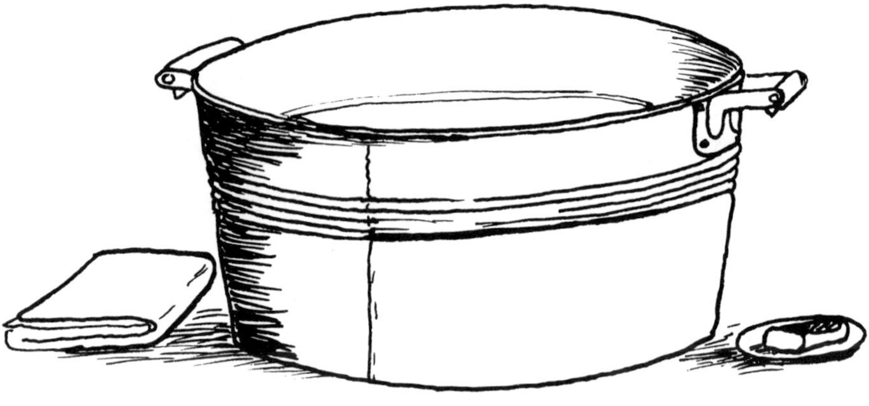

Wash Tub

Christmas, 1938 Style

Christmas was coming in less than one week. Mother told Father to put up the tree in our living room that everyone called the parlor in those days. He dutifully went about finding a twelve-quart pail and filled it with sand saved for this purpose before winter set in. He shaped the end of the tree to a point with a hand saw, and he then set the tree into the sand and made a wood brace to fit into the pail to support it. He carried the tree into the parlor and said he would add water when we had decorated it.

Our tree was, as always, a spruce, the most common and least expensive kind. It was freshly cut, but even so, it would drop a lot of needles before we took it down in three weeks.

Mother supervised my sister and me in decorating it. We had strung a short length of popped corn a day or two earlier, and the only other rope was a thin, glittery gold rope that had come from Grandma Inger's house on the adjacent farm. With these two ropes in place Mother and Hazel hung the glass balls of many colors. I handed the delicate balls to them one at a time, for I was not permitted to remove the tiny wire loop and hang them on the twigs until I was older.

Mother was very tall, but she had to really stretch hard to top the tree with a tall spire of colored glass mounted on a round bulb. It was shaped like the finials on an old-fashioned poster bed.

Then we girls each stood on a chair to hang our six-inch, red-felt Santas near the top. These were gifts received as toddlers when we still had faith in Santa Claus.

While Hazel and I hung silver tinsel one at a time on the very tips of the twigs, Mother fastened our twelve candleholders on the outer ends of the branches, safely away from anything that could burn. She put four-inch red candles in them. These would be lit and burned only on Christmas Eve. The tree would be too dry after that and the fire hazard too great. Electric lights on the tree were yet unheard of where we lived.

Imagine a tree standing in a dark corner of a parlor illuminated only by a kerosene lamp! We did have a mantle over our lamp wick which gave off a whiter light than that of an ordinary wick lamp. One can easily understand that shiny tinsel and glass balls were popular because they caught the light beautifully. The felt Santas, on the other hand, were barely visible by lamplight.

Mother cleaned the entire house to shiny perfection during those last days before Christmas Eve. Washing the walls and ceilings for Christmas was an old Norwegian tradition, but we had a new bungalow with walls and ceilings of plaster rather than painted wood boards. These could not be washed, so Mother went over the surfaces with a new broom covered with a dust cloth and swept down any cobwebs that had mysteriously appeared. She carefully wiped the dust from the picture moulding which was a varnished wooden strip around the entire room about one foot from the ceiling. All pictures hung by wire from hooks over this moulding. It was a great dust catcher. Then the six-inch tall baseboards around every room had to be dusted off and polished. Dusting and polishing the furniture seemed to be the easiest part.

Without a doubt the worst cleaning jobs were the stoves. The cookstove had to be cleaned inside and out and then blackened with a commercial blackening agent which required lots of elbow grease. The pot-bellied heating stove burned coal, so one simply shook the grates and shoveled out the ashes into a pail, and the inside was considered clean. But one had to carefully wash and dry each tiny square of isinglass through which we could watch the flames dance in blue, red and white over the burning coal. The entire stove surface was rubbed, and the decorative chrome trim had to be polished until it shone. How we were admonished to keep our fingers off!

The last cleaning job in our farm home was to dust mop the wood floors and wash the linoleum-covered ones. The kitchen and entry floors were scrubbed with a husky brush and soapy water.

Father appeared in the doorway with a stack of split oak firewood for the kitchen range just as Mother started washing the kitchen floor. The wood was piled on one arm and stacked to his eyebrows. It was a wonder he could see where to walk. He got down on one knee and put the chunks into the woodbox which was a permanent fixture in the kitchen. He had hurried to do this before she washed the floor because it always littered the floor with chips of wood and small blobs of snow. He knew that she had worked hard and was tired by now, and he knew how to keep the peace on Christmas Eve.

Christmas supper was being prepared even as the floor was being scrubbed. I remember the fresh scent of the evergreen tree and the sweet aroma of furniture polish mingling with cooking odors from the pork ribs baking in the oven, and later, the *lutefisk* simmering in a kettle on top of the kitchen range.

Father had gone to the barn to finish his evening chores, and at last supper was ready just as he came in and cleaned up at the sink under the cistern pump in the kitchen. He added some hot water from the shiny tea kettle on the stove to the cold cistern water and washed his face and hands. Then he put on clean denim overalls in honor of the occasion.

When we were seated at the kitchen table, Mother served the boiled potatoes, ribs, *lutefisk*, melted butter for the *lutefisk*, and some carrots. There was also brown bread called *grov brød* and lots of my favorite food, *lefse*.

I always ate very little, and the nervous anticipation of Christmas and gifts under the tree caused me to eat even less. Mother understood this and did not force the issue, letting me eat a snack before going to bed.

When our plates were empty, we were served a saucedish of *søtsuppe*, meaning sweet soup. It was not soup at all, but rather a thin sauce of dried prunes, raisins, pears, and apricots cooked in water with a tad of vinegar and some sugar. Mother usually added a little sago to give it body. Sago was round and smooth and fun to eat, but it was quite tasteless. It was similar to tapioca and was then a common food.

Waiting for my parents to finish eating so that we could open our presents was almost unbearable. Father really liked those ribs, and Mother ate voraciously of *lutefisk*. At long last they got up from the table and left the dishes unwashed.

First, by family tradition, Mother lit the candles on the tree as Father turned down the wick on the mantle lamp to darken the room. Hazel and I savored this glorious moment for perhaps five minutes. We stood back and counted the shiny balls on the tree. Could we find them all in the dim light of the room? As beautiful as the brief display was, we didn't mind when Mother wet her thumb and pointer finger to pinch out the tiny flames because opening our gifts was the very next activity.

As I watched her, I thought about the first book I had received—an ABC book for preschoolers with a full-page black-and-white picture to go with each letter. I had treasured it. Another book given to me two years later was a fat, square Little Orphan Annie book. My favorite toy was a metal red-headed woodpecker with a big, ugly key sticking out from its back. One could wind up the spring and watch the bird noisily peck the floor as it traveled in circles. I still have it and it still works. It seemed I had always been interested in birds, and birdwatching had become a real pastime for me. So I was hoping to get a bird identification book I had seen at Woolworth's Five and Dime in Fergus Falls. It was about three inches tall and six inches wide, and I hoped my parents could afford it.

A child isn't very concerned about what anyone else gets, especially the adults. I'm sure that my mother's only gift for many years was a pair of new felt slippers to cozy her feet from the cold wood floors. Father usually got a pair of heavy wool socks.

Hazel and I got three packages each that year. I got to play Santa and pass out the gifts because my sister was now older and no longer wanted to do that. I gave a package to her and took one for myself. Hers turned out to be a game of checkers; mine a set of Old Maid cards.

Would I get that bird book I had hinted about? I hurried for another gift for each of us. My sister got something of no interest to me, so I can't recall what it was. I carefully unwrapped my gift, quite sure it was too large to be that tiny book. As I unrolled the contents, the coveted book appeared, as well as one on wild flowers and one on freshwater fish. It was like three gifts, and my joy was complete.

There remained two boxes the size and shape of shoe boxes, so we knew before we opened them that we were getting new slippers again. We eagerly put them on.

Some stores used colorful wrapping paper at Christmas time, but we never purchased gift wrap. We did not rip it or crumple it as we unwrapped our presents. Instead, we folded the colored wrapping paper very carefully and treasured it almost as much as a gift. After hoarding it for days or weeks, Mother put it away in a closet for reuse the next year.

I was deliriously happy the rest of the evening. We enjoyed playing with our games and then shelled and ate peanuts and had more *lefse* and milk before going to bed. Mother did the dishes while Father sat with one ear to the speaker of his car battery-operated radio.

I lay in bed thinking of the wonderful time we'd had. I felt secure and loved, sensing somehow the devotion of my parents in their collective efforts in making Christmas Eve a special time. In a very short time I fell asleep, knowing there would be fresh doughnuts and an apple and a little hard candy in my stocking in the morning.

We Go Julebukk

Norwegian communities followed Christmas with an evening of *Julebukking*. This custom was perhaps as traditional in Minnesota as in Norway when I was a child.

I first experienced *Julebukking* at the age of four. My mother's kerosene lamp was lit and was standing in the middle of our square oak dining table where I was coloring or drawing something. I intuitively looked out the window to my right and saw in the darkness a masked face and a human form which came close up to the window. Even though I instantly recognized the person from his general appearance as our neighbor's hired man, fear gripped me. I felt a chill down my spine as I flew around the table into the kitchen. I sat down, cowering, on a fifteen-dozen egg case which made an ideal seat for me. I felt some sense of security there, away from the window and in a corner. Mother was also nearby in the kitchen. By now she was chuckling and opening the kitchen door to let in the group of five masked and somewhat costumed adults.

The five spoke not a word but gestured to indicate hunger. While Mother went to fetch a doughnut for each, Father teased them with inflammatory remarks to get them to speak. My sister joined in at guessing who they were and at trying to get them to speak. As was the custom, the ones correctly identified had to lift up or remove their masks. That was an unwritten rule of *Julebukking*. Then they could eat their treats. Their masks were all home-made, usually by cutting holes for eyes and nose in a flour sack and painting around the holes.

When the identity of all was revealed, they thanked us noisily and went on to another farm to scare more unsuspecting children. Scaring small fry was not the intention, but to this very day I am uncomfortable and insecure sitting by a window in an illuminated room without the drapes drawn. I seem to expect to see a face out there.

Jul means Christmas, and *bukk* is a goat buck. Sometime between Christmas and Epiphany it was the custom in Norway and also in Norse populated parts of America to go *Julebukking*. It goes back to ancient times in Norway when society there placed great importance on timely Christmas preparations. No work was to be done once Christmas had come. A goat-being would hang around ready to punish anyone who got out of line.

The revelers carried the hand-made head of a Christmas goat from house to house. This was the *Julebukk.*

In early times some came costumed as goats. This deteriorated to today's *Julebukkers* wearing any costume and facial disguise. People have forgotten the origins of *Julebukking*, but have fun doing it anyhow.

Several years later I went *Julebukking* on skis with three other young people. It was a bright, moonlit night, and the weather was perfect. A bachelor with a suspicious nature threatened us with a shotgun as he ordered us off his property, but then he wasn't Norwegian. We stuck to Norwegians after that, and all those we visited joined in our fun.

Lutefisk, Lefse, Klubb

We always had *lutefisk* for Christmas. Norwegian fishermen long ago learned to dry their codfish by splitting them along the spine and hanging them on racks in the fresh outdoor air. Then they learned to soak these pieces in a lye solution to make them fluff out for eating. The lye preserved the flesh which would soon spoil without refrigeration.

Mother soaked *lutefisk* in clear water at least twice to get rid of as much lye taste as possible. Then she boiled it gently in salted water and served it at once with boiled potatoes and melted butter. If it were Christmas, we also had pork ribs.

Everyone in Minnesota has at least heard of *lefse*, which is made from mashed potatoes mixed with flour and a bit of shortening, salt and sugar. It is mixed when cold and rolled out as thin as possible and baked on a hot surface. In those days Mother put the *lefse* pieces right onto the kitchen range surface. When one side showed light brown spots, she turned it over with a flattened wooden stick. It was served with butter and a sprinkle of sugar, all rolled up. To this day I prefer summer sausage or weiners with *lefse*.

Klubb was a dumpling made quite solid and large, the size of baseballs. Many Norwegians took blood from the animal being butchered and mixed it with flour to make *blod-klubb* (blood dumplings). It sounds unappetizing now, even barbaric! This *klubb* was boiled in water until thoroughly cooked inside. When the *blod-klubb* was cool, Mother cut it into inch-size cubes and heated it in a heavy fry pan with a bit of bacon fat. It tasted like meat. It was the most delicious food of all time, or so I thought then.

Today if you wish to try *klubb* minus the blood, some Minnesota communities, notably Benson, serve *klubb* one day a week in their restaurants. It is usually served with sausage or bologna.

Everyday sweets eaten most often during the Depression years were plain cake and oatmeal rocks. Plain cake was made of flour, eggs, baking powder, milk and sugar. Cinnamon and white sugar could be sprinkled over the cake; sometimes a glaze of powdered sugar and water was spread on top. Oatmeal rocks are oatmeal drop cookies with raisins, and I still make them often.

On Sunday afternoons the bowl of red Jello gelatin with bananas sliced into it and whipped cream on top showed up on most tables for guests if the hostess could afford it.

A Norwegian hostess always served much more food than the guests could possibly eat. It was considered hospitable to offer several choices. Thus my aunts' tables were covered with frosted layer cakes, a frosted angel food cake, doughnuts, at least three kinds of cookies, buns, cheese, jam, Jello, and pear or peach sauce. All this was homemade from scratch or home-canned. If the guests didn't try almost every kind of food, the hostess thought her food lacked appeal. The host family also had to eat all the leftovers over the next several days.

My mother thought all this fuss and waste of food was foolish, so she greatly limited her lunches.

I hated this huge meal of desserts because I had a small appetite, and I hated having adults hang over me and beg me to eat.

When I wanted a snack at home, I put a slice of white bread on a plate and covered it with cold cream and some Karo syrup and ate that. Karo syrup was inexpensive and came in one-gallon metal pails with a cover and handle. All the school children carried their lunches to school in them during the '30's.

House Guest

One cold April Fool's Day morning when I was perhaps ten years old, my mother was in the kitchen, not cooking, but cutting my father's hair. He had only a rim of hair as the top of his head was totally bald. In the '30's no one on a farm paid a barber to have a haircut, at least not those who were bald.

While this was going on, Mother asked him, "Why did you go into the basement after chores last night?" It was just a casual question born of curiosity.

"I wasn't in the basement last night. I wasn't in the basement all day yesterday," was his reply.

"But the girls and I heard you go down the steps."

"You couldn't have heard me because I wasn't in the basement," he repeated.

There were claims and counter claims made as we two girls added our comments siding with Mother. It got to be a rather heated argument, and nothing got resolved.

I was sure that Father had gone into the basement. When we had been preparing for bed the night before, we had procrastinated beyond our bedtime which was 9:00 p.m. Our bedroom was beside the back door to the house, so it was easy to hear anyone entering or exiting. At about 9:20 we had all three clearly heard the squeaking of the hinges on the storm door and the following thud of each footstep down the stairs leading to the basement floor. Mother had said urgently, "John's coming in from the barn now. Hurry and get into bed!" We had obeyed and Mother had blown out the light from the kerosene lamp.

As soon as Mother finished trimming Father's hair, she put away the comb and clipper and went into the basement to get a jar of peaches for our noon meal. After a prolonged moment of silence down there she shouted up the steps for Father to come down at once. He did so, followed by two curious daughters.

There on the basement floor lay Father's fleece-lined overcoat spread out neatly with the fleece side up. At the head end lay folded an old, worn quilt. On it was a visible indentation from someone's head. It was obvious that someone had slept there, and Father now believed our statement that we had heard the door open and had heard the footsteps of someone walking down the stairs.

Then Father remembered that when he had gone out to the barn that morning, the storm door was ajar a couple inches. It was his habit to hook the door shut at night with a small hook fastened at eye level. The intruder had not tried to avoid being heard when he entered, so it is doubtful he left early to avoid disturbing us. Even though we had a new house with a full basement, we had no furnace, and the uninvited guest had no doubt found it rather chilly down there.

This story was told to all our friends and neighbors. We had a suspicion that it was a prank since it happened the night before April Fool's Day. No explanation ever came to light, but I cannot believe that a neighbor walking in so boldly or pulling off this practical joke so successfully would never tell anyone about it. Who it was—neighbor, peddler, tramp, criminal or an escapee from the mental hospital—we will never know. I have often wondered what might have happened had Mother gone to the basement that night to talk to her husband.

Since this experience, the door was always locked at night at our house, and I lock my doors to this very day.

Spring, a Time of Renewal

The arrival of spring seed catalogs in the mail had always tempted my mother to drop whatever she was doing to start planning her garden and beds of flowers. The catalogs came as early as February, but it didn't matter that we usually got two or three blustery periods and sometimes a blizzard before we could actually plant anything; she had the craving to get going with planning and ordering right away. I am, in this respect, truly my mother's daughter.

Faith is always there: faith that the temperature will soon hold above freezing; faith that the snow will soon thaw and cease to fall. Crocuses push their showy heads through the black soil before April's Fools Day and are followed by tulips in what is my favorite season of the year. Early spring shows off green lawns against naked, brown, deciduous woods with stubborn, dirty snowdrifts among the tree trunks. Tulips and green lawns are incredibly rich and crisp in color, making the world look bright and clean. The earth is washed by spring rains that bring out the heavenly scent of fruit trees in bloom.

Growing flowers in a flower bed was a simple hobby in the '30's. I never heard of anyone raising crocuses or tulips then. We saved seeds from dry annuals in the fall to plant the next spring without having to purchase the seeds. It was easy to keep zinnias, cosmos, or petunias going with home-produced seed, and hollyhocks perpetuated themselves. If one desired a new kind of flower, one asked a friend or neighbor for seed or a root. Irises and peonies were thus spread around the community.

The difficult part was watering. Water was scarce during periods of drought, and farms did not have running water which meant that water had to be hand-pumped from a cistern or well and carried in pails to the flowers or garden. When "victory gardens" were encouraged by the federal government during the '40's, farm women really struggled to keep a vegetable garden weeded and watered.

Spring meant hard work and extra work, but we found ourselves looking forward to trees leafing out, to new calves and kittens, and later on, to aromatic alfalfa hay.

Nearly every farmer in Minnesota in the '30's and '40's brought home baby chicks from the local hatchery, usually in March or early April. What excitement there was in lifting the tiny, feather-weight, peeping chicks from their cardboard carton onto the floor covered with chipped corn cobs, or commercial litter! They would hesitate only a moment before darting around the room in the sheer joy of having room to run after a night spent in their cramped paper carton with the round peep holes.

When the chicks settled down, they ate their fill and drank water from the inverted glass jug water fountains. Then they stood huddled under the light and warmth of the brooder stove canopy, lying down at last to sleep as a group, tiny body to tiny body, eyelids drooping and little heads tucked into their fluffy down. It was very important to have the temperature just right to prevent their crowding one another and piling up, causing death.

My favorite spring joy as a child was to hatch out 30 to 40 white Pekin ducklings. This was my project and my income, but mostly it was my favorite pastime. I kept two or three adult hens and one drake over winter. They survived, even thrived, in an unheated log shed. Ducks can take very cold temperatures if they have dry bedding to keep their feet warm, and if they have plenty of cracked corn to eat for body warmth.

Hens hatched out their fluffy, yellow ducklings after 28 patient days on the nest. I transferred them to a pen outdoors where they could run on fresh grass. In the pen I put a "house" which had a triangular plywood board at the back and a two-way roof that came forward from this board and formed walls that ran from the top of the triangle to the ground on both sides.

Ducklings are very comical creatures. They love to slop in water or to stand out in gentle rain, neither of which they can take in big doses, so I was sure to shut them into their shelter at night and during rainy periods. There they slept under their mother's warm body. Drafts and chills are to be avoided as they can bring on a cold which usually causes death.

Ducklings have more fun while eating than any critter I know. They stand and joyously slop around in their feed pans, filling their bills with wet mash (moistened ground grain) and hurrying over to a water pan to swish water through their food and to drink. Back to the feed they go, repeating the trip to the water with a full bill. They must have wet mash because they would choke on dry grain.

Ducklings waddle comically and make a sort of giggling sound that seems to say, "dig-ah-tick." They are easily tamed if one is patient and slow in one's movements around them, and they quickly learn to respond to one's call. If they are hungry, they will come running as rapidly as their little legs can churn. They are cheerful and communicative.

Poultry and gardens do not go well together. Ducks love lettuce, and mature chickens love to bathe in loose, dry garden soil, so it can be a problem keeping poultry out of a garden.

My mother kept a large garden near the house. It was fenced with wire mesh fencing to keep the poultry and dogs out. Some determined chickens bathed in the dry soil beside the fence until they undermined the fence and got into the garden. No matter how large the hole they created, they could never manage to find the hole to get out again.

One day Mother chased a wily white rock hen around and around in the garden for nearly a half-hour before catching her up against a large pail. Upon catching her, Mother swung that hen by the legs in a full circle in the air before letting her go over the fence top.

Plop! The dizzy chicken dropped straight down on the hard driveway to her instantaneous death. Screeching brakes brought the approaching cream truck to a halt just as the chicken landed in front of the truck bumper. Both were unexpected developments.

A surprised cream hauler and my astonished and somewhat red-faced mother were in conference over the dead chicken no more than five seconds. The gentleman grabbed a handy axe and did what needed doing while mother went for two pails of hot water. She then plucked the feathers, and we later enjoyed stewed chicken and dumplings for supper.

Horse jockeys made their rounds in the spring before farmers got into the fields, if possible. A jockey traveled alone, on foot, leading as many as four or five horses, and on rare occasion, six horses, as he walked from farm to farm. The jockey would ask permission to water the horses at the watering tank. Permission was granted, and usually they drank it so dry that Father would start the gasoline engine to pump more water.

Then there followed a lively dickering between the jockey and my father. Most often the jockey left, no richer for the time spent but for a quick sandwich or a free meal. The jockeys truly lived off the land. There was no place to buy food, and some farmers were too poor to offer them food, so some days were days of starvation for the jockey.

Sometimes they purchased a horse from the farmer, if they hoped to gain by it, but it was barter plus cash that they were after. They purchased only when they sensed a good deal in the making, hoping to sell their purchase down the road soon.

As for their selling ability, let the buyer beware. Few farmers in the Great Depression could afford to purchase a horse, so they aimed to trade for a better one. It became a game of wits: a matter of who could better judge a horse's body conformation and temperament; of who could ferret out the best financial deal. My father bought at least four horses by barter over the years and sold a few as well. Some of them were ding-a-lings one way or another.

One such horse followed me wherever I went. He seemed harmless as a puppy until one foggy day when I wanted to go to the next farm to visit my school chum. I didn't know that he was loose in our yard when I left home, so I was surprised when his huge form suddenly loomed behind me in the fog. I was by then crossing a plowed field, and I stopped and yelled at him. He only tossed his head. I picked up clumps of black dirt and threw at him. He reared. I threw a small rock and struck him in the chest. Then he took a few steps toward me and reared on his hind feet, pawing the air as he shinnied right above my head. His flailing hooves missed me as they came down hard only two feet in front of me! Terrified, I turned and ran, and he followed. I had no place to go for protection, so I made a big circle and returned home with the horse right at my heels. I learned that night that he had pulled this threat on my father, too, so the next horse jockey to come around got him in a trade.

Two and three generations ago, spring also brought out the walking peddler. One such salesman who visited our farm in the '30's was a droopy-shouldered, elderly Norwegian whose name was Sigvart Maaseby. One would look up from one's outdoor work to see Sigvart's familiar form stumbling his way across the neighbor's plowed field while carrying his heavy black bag in which he carried spices, cleaners, and "Rosen Pudder," a rose-scented talcum powder that was supposed to make a lady smell as fresh as a summer garden. Sigvart Maaseby was a most unlikely cosmetic salesman.

Sigvart usually came in late April, but one year he failed to appear. It was already June, and he had not come. We were beginning to speculate on what may have happened to him when the lumbering form of the old peddler appeared across the field.

On that day Mother had just washed and trimmed a bowl of radishes from the garden, at least four cups full. The radishes were in the center of the table as Sigvart came in. As soon as he saw them he let out an exclamation of joy and asked permission to taste them.

"*Vaer saa god!* (Help yourself!)" Mother said as she offered him a chair at our table. She proceeded to make a pot of fresh coffee and to get out some doughnuts.

I sat down across the table from Sigvart and observed his noisy crunching and smacking as he devoured one crisp radish after another.

"*Dem er helsy. Dem er god!* (They are wholesome. They are good!)" he said in American-Norwegian as he enthusiastically munched each radish. Sooner than Mother could get the coffee ready, he had eaten them all!

After a cup or two of coffee and a couple of doughnuts, and after selling Mother a bottle of vanilla and trying unsuccessfully to get her to buy some Rosen Pudder, he left and walked westward to the next neighbor.

I often wondered how far he got before the coffee, radishes and doughnuts did battle, giving him an acute attack of heartburn!

In and Out the Lilacs

A wide row of tall lilac bushes grew along the driveway that ran past our house. Here I played, usually alone, with a wooden coffee grinder that no one yet cherished as an antique. I ground ripe acorns in it to use as pretend coffee for my pretend guests. I had separate rooms among the trunks of the bushes, completely shaded and isolated from the outside world by the lush, green foliage. Here I made cupboards from two-pound wooden cheese boxes. Sometimes I ate raw acorns or thorn-apples, and I made nectar. We didn't have Kool Aid then, but we bought extracts from the traveling Watkins or McConnon peddlers and made nectar with extract, sugar and water. When I wasn't hungry I made mud pies, mud muffins and mud cookies in play tins I had gotten for Christmas.

My lilac house was the sweetest-smelling place in the world when the lilacs were in bloom, especially after a light rain. It was also cooler in there during hot weather. Privacy permitted me to talk aloud to my pretend guests.

We had a wild hawthorn tree in our pasture which everyone called a thornapple tree. Its fruit was small, round and smooth, and orange in color when ripe. It was meaty and solid, somewhat like eating the inner flesh of orange peel. We girls made *neverskrukker* to hold the thornapples we picked.

Neverskrukker is a Norwegian word, in the plural form. *Never* is birch, and *skrukkker* are small basket-like containers. A triangular piece of birchbark could be cut and curved into the shape of a cone, then stitched together along the edge to form a cone-shaped cup. We used young, pliable willow stems to "stitch" the sides where I had punched holes with a small nail. These doubled as cups in my pretend kitchen.

Sometimes during the summer small groups of Gypsies walked or drove a car into our yard. If I was out-of doors when they were seen approaching, I ran to my lilac hideaway and stayed hidden until they were gone. We feared them as we had heard tales of their thievery and worse behavior. Mother usually hurried to give them a loaf of bread or a quart jar of cold, fresh milk. They always thanked us and left, never stealing anything. I think they may have stolen food when they were desperate and were not offered anything, but we never had difficulty with them. The Depression years were as rough for them as for anyone else.

Those lilac bushes also hold a very funny memory for me. Uncle Edwin lived on the Ekeberg family farm adjacent to ours. As was customary, cows were led to the neighbor farm for breeding if they were related to the sire on the farm where they lived. I looked out from the lilac bushes where I was playing one day to see what the ruckus was about, and I saw Uncle Edwin approaching, leading a big Guernsey on a rope halter. It was easy to see she wasn't exactly halter broke, and I barely had time to scramble out of the lilacs to run to the safety of the back porch. Obviously, the cow was leading Uncle Edwin, not the other way around.

Suddenly Bossie bolted and took off right through the row of lilacs which at that time were about six feet tall. Edwin hung onto the lead rope with both hands, digging in his heels ahead of him and leaning way back with his head turned sharply to the left and his eyes shut tightly. Bossie dragged him through the entire length of the lilac row, at least thirty feet of lilacs, trying to get rid of him. A lesser man would have dropped the rope, but despite losing his glasses and getting multiple scratches from the woody branches, it appeared Edwin might come out the victor at the far end.

The cow had her eyes shut as well when she cleared the last bush. She came out bellowing, and Edwin was muttering and calling the cow evil names. He still had a grip on that rope so that Bossie had to come along to the barn.

Meanwhile I had gone into a real fit of uncontrollable laughter, and I found Mother standing beside me, laughing, too. Mother told me to find Edwin's glasses, which I did–hanging unbroken on one of the first branches.

I surveyed the wreckage of my secret rooms. Many things were tipped over or smashed, but the precious coffee grinder survived unscathed.

I rescued the coffee grinder when we moved from the farm, and it now sits on my dining room hutch, saved for posterity—a memorial to my childhood, to Uncle Edwin, and to the Gypsies.

Shivarees and Mock Weddings

My husband and I must be among the last couples in our area to have been shivareed by our neighbors outside our bedroom window our first night home after the honeymoon. At least we haven't heard of this being done for anyone else since the 1940's.

That night, a half hour after we had gone to bed, we were jarred out of our sleep by a loud serenade outside our window. Cooking ladles banged repeatedly on sturdy frying pans, rocks tossed about in covered kettles, and dangling tin cans made music like a string of cow bells. Kettle covers clashed together like cymbals. It was not unlike the first practice session of an elementary school rhythm band, but without as much rhythm and with even more noise.

A shivaree was the customary thing to do in the 1930's. It was cheap entertainment for the performers because the newly-weds were expected to invite the unwanted guests in for beverage and food. Obviously, the performers enjoyed it much more than the couple who were shivareed.

Where this mad custom began, I do not know. But the original word was *charivari*, and it meant to drive the victims to madness by noise of the mob.

During the Great Depression my father employed a very soft-spoken, shy, but loyal hired man named Lester who did farm chores and field work for room and board and very little pay. He must have been about 30 years old when he fell in love with the neighbor's hired girl, Pearl.

Lester and Pearl were about the same age, both from poor homes, and both lacked education beyond being able to read. This was not unusual in that time when very few adults where I grew up had gone to high school and everyone was poor; it was just a question of how poor.

Lester and Pearl courted by going for walks down a nearby dirt road on Saturday evenings until Lester managed to buy a used Model T Ford.

One hot summer afternoon after working over a stubborn motor for hours with no luck in starting the engine, Lester let loose all his pent-up frustration over not being able to locate the problem that kept him from calling on Pearl on time. He impulsively yanked the timer from under the hood and heaved it in a mighty burst of anger way over the treetops! I heard it land somewhere in the underbrush, completely out of sight. Lester then stuck his head under the hood and set forth pounding and cursing away.

About that time my father came home from the fields. He put the team of horses into the barn and contributed his mechanical expertise to the problem at hand. Father soon concluded that the timer was not the cause of the malfunction, and in short order I was sent to fetch the timer from out of the brush.

Fighting gooseberry bushes, chokecherry brush, and tangled vines, I searched for the timer until I found it, wires sticking out from it in all directions.

But my father managed to install it again and repair whatever was wrong. Lester was very late, but he did get to see Pearl. It so happened that it was on this emotionally-charged night that Pearl agreed to marry Lester.

The next day while Father and Lester were pitching manure out of the barn, they discussed the matter of an engagement ring. A diamond was out of Lester's league. My father half-jokingly told Lester that he could always find a fake diamond and a gold band at Woolworth's in Fergus Falls.

A week later, Lester presented Pearl with a ring, boxed and resting on cotton. It had a gold-colored band with a fake diamond, and I can only guess what went through the mind of the store clerk at Woolworth's when Lester picked it out.

The couple decided to wed some weeks later at the Otter Tail County courthouse, that being the most affordable way to go. But first, new clothing was in order, clothing that they could not afford.

My father showed great compassion and trust when he sacked up a load of oats for Lester to sell at the elevator on the promise that he would work off the debt. My mother helped by finding an ad in the *Fergus Falls Daily Journal* calling attention to a smoke sale in an unlucky clothing store. She suggested they go there.

Lester got a real bargain: an all-wool suit that looked great for only $5. My mother shortened the trousers by several inches and pressed the suit. She didn't have to do a thing with Pearl's new orange-and-green plaid wool dress.

Pearl and Lester were married in their finery and contributed a dollar tip to the official who performed the ceremony.

The next day the couple came home to attend their mock wedding. People filled the township hall. Friends and neighbors sat on the benches behind Pearl and Lester seated in the front row.

The largest and bravest man in the neighborhood strode up the aisle to the strains of "Here Comes the Bride." He wore a crown made of bindweed perched jauntily on his balding head. He also carried a bouquet of bull thistles and burdock, symbols of the worst a farmer's bride could imagine.

His "bride's" gown was fashioned from two panels of lace curtains, straining at the seams. A low neckline revealed a seed corn necklace above a well-padded bosom. A tattered cheesecloth, taken perhaps from the nearest raspberry patch, made up the train, and the bride's hairy ankles were revealed between the slit in the curtains and the tops of a pair of high-top laced boots.

At the bride's side walked a shriveled little groom played by the frailest old lady who would volunteer for such tomfoolery.

A fake mustache and beard added masculinity to her wrinkled face; her gray hair, pulled back in a bun, hid beaneath an old beaver top hat. A soloist belted out the song, "My Good-looking Man."

There were bridesmaids in bib overalls and groomsmen in longjohns. I was the flower girl dropping dandelions in the aisle. The buxom parson, a middle-aged lady dressed in high-water trousers and an undersized suitcoat, delivered a hilarious version of the traditional wedding vows followed by a lengthy sermon on how to stay married through thick and thin. Mostly thin.

And what did Pearl and Lester think of the spoof? They practically choked with laughter all the way through the mock wedding.

A potluck lunch was served afterward, and for Pearl and Lester the finest wedding reception would not have pleased them more. This was the way the community could show their affection for the couple, one of the few ways anyone could afford in the Depression years. Everyone wished Pearl and Lester the best.

I doubt if Pearl cared that there was no gold or diamond in her ring.

To Be or Not to Be Beautiful

Two single aunts and a bachelor uncle lived on the Ekeberg family farm adjacent to ours, and their sisters, Alma and Inga, were beauticians in Minneapolis and frequently came home to visit. I remember them dressed in the stylish sleeveless, straight-cut, long-waisted dresses with short pleated skirts that the flappers of the '20's and early '30's are remembered for. Long strands of pearls or other spangles decorated the neckline or hung down the plain front of the dress. This was the dress to wear when dancing the Charleston.

These aunts wore the latest in clothing styles, and they were the first ladies I ever saw wearing slacks. Girls began to wear summer "pajamas," a one-piece dress-up version of the night pajama, when I was about five years old. Slacks became popular sometime after that. Aunt Inga wore her slacks as tight as possible, and when she bent over, the seams groaned to hold together.

Inga was once called on by a suitor who showed up in his Model T touring car with side curtains, wearing a dark suit, dress shirt, tie, and light gray, buttoned spats over his patent leather dress shoes. Everyone laughed at him and called him a "dandy" after he left.

Hazel and I visited these aunts when they came home. When I was four or five years old, they put Hazel into a chair and proceeded to set her hair with lots of sticky wave set and metal wave clamps. They were experts at making large waves with a comb and their fingers, and they made tight round spit curls around the face. This style of repeated large waves was called a fingerwave.

Soon it was my turn. But I recalled suffering under the hands of Mother and her hot curling iron all too often to be interested in this! The curling iron was heated by inverting it into a kerosene lamp chimney over the flame. My ears had suffered painful water blisters many times when I could not sit still long enough as Mother tried to curl my short hair. So, I refused the only offer I ever had to get a fingerwave.

Some years later, Hazel was a budding teenager and wanted her first real permanent. I was curious and wanted to come along to watch. Father drove us to Battle Lake, and whether he waited or came back for us I can't recall.

Hazel's hair was very thick and quite coarse. The question

*Heat Clamps for Permanenting Hair ,
on Display at Pope County Historical Museum*

was whether there would be enough heat elements with clamps to fit over the curlers. These electric heat clamps were each attached to a cord about 18 inches long that was attached to a stand, all looking like a floor lamp with 28 curler clamps.

The beautician gave her a shampoo and divided the hair into sections as she worked, putting a curler in each section. In a short time she could see that the sections would have to contain more hair in each if there were to be enough clamps, so she removed the curlers and combed it out to try again.

The second attempt seemed to go well, especially as they were busy visiting. When she finished the job on one side, she counted the curlers. This still used too many, so she removed the curlers and did the thicker part of the hair first down the center of the head. This would surely take care of the problem.

You guessed it. She had still used too many curlers. In fact she was almost out of curlers as well as heat clamps.

We all three had a refreshing, cold glass of water while a conference was held between beautician and paying customer. It was decided to remove all the curlers and put them on one side of the head only, permanenting that half, then winding up the hair on the other side and permanenting that separately.

I have never had a more miserable day trying to sit still, waiting. I suffered from boredom, a sore seat, and hunger. Five hours had gone by. I took one look at the bird's nest appearance of my sister's hair when she finally got ready to go home, and I decided against beauty parlors then and there. Consequently, I cut and curled my own hair with home permanent kits until I was 50 years old! To be or not to be beautiful? This was no question.

Meeting My Savior

My father was uneducated and knew very little about the background of the Bible. He had little or no idea who had written the various books, and he was sure that Martin Luther had written some of it, being the loyal Lutheran that he was. He could quote many Bible verses and knew at least some of the stories from the Bible. Most important, he was a firm believer in Christ the Savior.

Mother's parents had arrived from Norway as members of the Lutheran State Church, but the ministers preached mostly hellfire-and-damnation sermons in those days, according to my grandpa, and he sought a more working faith that preached the love of God and the benefits of living a moral life. They sought to disassociate themselves from regular Lutheranism.

Religion became a topic that was taboo in our home. It was a topic that produced conflict. I was not taken to Sunday School as a young child, and we seldom went to Sunday services. When I was eleven, Aunt Anna on the adjacent farm approached my mother about sending me to Sunday School in the Skiptvet Church about three miles away. Mother decided to send me.

My father took turns with Roger's father getting us there by car until Roger began to drive us in a Model A Ford. I think he was only thirteen when he began to drive. We attended Sunday School in the warm season and through Christmas, then again in the late spring. Roger's brother and a neighbor girl also rode with us.

God, Christ, the Savior, Redeemer, and Lord were all just words to me when I started. I knew about the baby Jesus of Christmas, but just what was accomplished on the cross or why the people crucified Jesus were things I had no understanding of. I knew that my father believed in God and in Jesus, and I didn't know just what my mother believed. She was the one, however, who arranged for me to attend Sunday School and to take Confirmation instruction, both in Lutheran churches.

My Sunday School teacher was a Mrs. Olson, and I liked her. The lady who was the superintendent was Miss Inga Berg, and she conducted the opening exercises, as we called the service the whole group had together. By the efforts of the two of them I learned the Gospel message of salvation and the meaning of all those confusing terms.

Miss Berg had asthma, and when it got cold in the church she began to wheeze something awful. We kids wanted to laugh about it, but we never lacked respect for her. Quite the contrary, we admired her for her devotion to teaching us despite her poor health and the miserable condition of that cold church.

I well remember one sunny morning when I walked home from Roger's house after Sunday School. I talked with God as I walked, and I prayed for whatever my teachers suggested that day. I recall praying for Jesus to be my teacher, companion, and savior. I prayed for forgiveness for my transgressions, and

I prayed for help in my daily life. I gave thanks for many blessings, naming them one by one. I felt a load of care lift from me as God took all my burdens unto Himself. I gained a working faith that is with me still, and I believe in the power of prayer and in the spiritual refreshment and insights one gets from reading the Bible. Three of my favorite hymns were introduced to me in Sunday School: "What a Friend We Have in Jesus," "Sweet Hour of Prayer," and "Jesus Savior Pilot Me."

I do not know whether there will be stars in my crown, but there will surely be stars for Mrs. Olson and Miss Berg.

"Will there be any stars, any stars in my crown
When at evening the sun goeth down?
When I wake with the blest in those mansions of rest,
Will there be any stars in my crown?"
Author Unknown

Wallpapering Mrs. Jones' House

Wood-frame outdoor toilets are almost impossible to find these days, but they flourished on farms and in villages until the 1940's. The ever-available Sears Roebuck and Montgomery Ward catalogs were in use then, too, in place of rolls of toilet tissue, a luxury only city folk had.

Our family toilet was built by a carpenter from Norway. It was a three-holer with vertical siding the way Norwegians built them. The rough-sawed oak boards were nearly a foot wide and an inch thick. They were placed an inch apart. Other boards on the inside were staggered to cover these inch-wide gaps, and they, too, were placed an inch apart. This made the double walls very solid and heavy. Definitely not the kind of biffy the kids could tip over on Halloween!

The door was less solid and had a slim quarter moon sawed into it about five feet up so that the adults could look out to see who drove into the yard.

One time my sister and I saved colorful calendar and magazine pictures for months, and on a sunny day we proceeded to wallpaper the toilet interior with them. Mixing a generous amount of flour and water for paste, we had a jolly time deciding on the arrangement of pictures and pasting them in place.

Horses, cats, sheep and pigs were hung beside Gene Autry, Amos and Andy, and the Dionne Quints. Joe Louis and Eleanore Roosevelt mingled with our favorite movie stars, Greer Garson and Walter Pidgeon. Little Orphan Annie was pasted just under the moon with Jack Armstrong, the All-American Boy, to her left and Charles Lindbergh to her right.

It was a fine job of wall papering, and it made "going to visit Mrs. Jones" a special pleasure.

Two days later when I entered the toilet in the morning, my heart sank. We had been visited by unwelcome guests. The vertical one-inch gaps in the walls were perfect crawl spaces for mice, and the flour paste was an unintentional invitation to feast and enjoy.

I'll never forget the total devastation. The mice had shredded our wallpaper everywhere along their inch-wide paths. An inch-wide strip even ran right up the middle of the gorgeous face of Loretta Young!

Papering had been fun, but Mother insisted that we remove the remains. That was something else!

Mrs. Jones' House

Joy and Danger at the Slough

"Supper! Come and eat!" Mother yelled.

At dusk during the summer when I was twelve years old, I was usually found beside the slough down from the big, red barn. I had acquired a three-inch long telescope through some offer on a cereal package, and with this I discovered the world of birds. I spent hours sitting in hiding behind some cattails watching hundreds of red-winged blackbirds and mallards. There were also special birds that I discovered there. I learned to know great blue herons, pintail ducks, American egrets, coots, and other birds I had never heard of. Mother had given me a dime-store bird identification book which was a great help, too.

Our slough had a lot of water in it, but the edge was rimmed by a strip at least twenty feet wide composed of clumps of grassy turf with black, wet mud between. I walked on these grassy clumps, and I once nearly stepped on a mature bittern standing among the cattails, bill pointed skyward. I froze, scarcely breathing, and admired it a minute before retreating to safer ground. It did not even fly up, so secure it was in its camouflage.

"Suppertime! Come home!" Mother called with greater authority in her voice.

I always started for home after the second round of calls. She must have worried about me walking beside the slough, or perhaps she did not know how daring I was. Cows seemed to manage walking among the grassy clumps to reach water, but our heavier horses sometimes sank into the mud and had to have help getting out.

Early one Easter morning in the mid-1940's I walked to the slough because it was snowing huge, heavy, wet flakes, and I wanted to enjoy the slough and the woods in the beauty of the snowfall. My joy gave way to fear when I discovered our big sorrel horse stuck in the mud. He was in deep, up to his chest.

I ran to tell Father, and by the time I finally found him and Mother in the barn, I was out of breath, my lungs stabbing with pain. I gasped out my message.

Father grabbed ropes and a couple of spades from our garage and hurried to bring his new Allis Chalmers tractor down to the slough. Mother quickly went to get our closest neighbor to help.

When he got down to the slough, my father patted the horse reassuringly and then furiously shoveled mud from around the horse's huge belly to try to get a rope under his body behind his front legs. It was a difficult, slow process. The neighbor came and began to shovel from the other side.

The minutes dragged by. It sickened me to think how this placid snowy scene had turned ugly, and I prayed for the horse and for the men who were also getting cold in the wet mud now plastered to their feet and legs. The men struggled for over an hour.

At long last Father's strong, long arm forced a rope under the horse's belly, and the man on the other side managed to grab the end, bringing it up to secure it on top. Another rope was put around the horse's neck. Many a horse had been rescued this way, so my hopes were high. Father attached the long ropes to the tractor's hitching bar, and then he began to pull slowly and gently.

This horse was in deeper and appeared to have been stuck longer than any other horse we had seen stuck before. He was very cold. He responded to the shouts of the men by struggling mightily to free himself, but the more he struggled, the deeper his body sank. There he lay after all the work and struggle, exhausted. All fight was gone from him.

More digging, more cursing the mud and the weather, more cold, wet snow. Another hour passed by as the men virtually dug a pit around the entire horse. The tractor pulled once more, and I feared the horse's head would snap right off at his neck. Finally the mud reluctantly gave way, and the limp body slithered out.

The big horse lay flat on his side beside the gaping hole. Mother and I hurried home for old quilts and warm water in pails. Father washed the cold mud from the horse's head, neck and chest and covered him with the quilts. Quite exhausted, everyone walked home. It did not look hopeful, but we could do no more. We thanked our good neighbor for his efforts. He was not offered pay. Neighbor helped neighbor in any emergency, and some day my father would be called upon to help him in turn. We went in to an overdone Easter dinner.

After eating only half-heartedly, I went with Father back to the slough to check on the horse. He lay motionless under the quilts while Father stooped to check. The big horse was dead.

I was sure the horse had seemed grateful for our efforts to save him, but that was a small comfort.

There was only one more thing to do on that cold, wet Easter

Sunday. My father hitched the tractor to the horse's hind legs and pulled him back into the slough, placing him in the same hole to sink deeper with time. There was no resurrection for the horse on that day.

From then on, although I continued to walk on the grassy tufts whenever I went birding, I was careful not to venture out as far toward the water.

District 45

Farm children were attending rural schools throughout the '30's and '40's in Minnesota. My sister and I walked almost a mile and a quarter each morning to get to our school, identified as District 45. For eight years we walked that road, but we went to school together for only four years because she was four grades ahead of me.

My first-grade teacher, who taught all the grades, was very ill-prepared. She spent her days yelling at the older boys who by law had to remain in school until they were sixteen or graduated, whichever occurred first. When she wasn't yelling, she was ducking wooden ABC blocks that they hurled across the room. Her basic problem was that she simply did not know how to teach, so her discipline fell apart.

I was a star pupil in my first grade class of eight, according to my Report Card to the Parents. At the end of the term it had nothing but A's on it for all subjects and all periods, but I had learned very little.

We started the second grade, and the new teacher discovered to her great dismay that she had on her hands a second grade class of eight virtual non-readers. Despite what the report cards said, only two of us had mastered the Pre Primer. She first lost her temper, slamming the second grade reading books onto the table followed by the first grade reading books. She tried some of us on the Primer, and they, too, were slammed onto the table. She then went to the storage closet and took out the Pre Primers, the phrase card chart, and the phonetic flash cards. We started again, from the beginning. She was, as my Norwegian parents put it, "a teacher with bone in her nose."

A fellow classmate, Henry, could understand English, but he had spoken Norwegian almost exclusively at home. It wasn't easy for him to think and speak in English. Before the end of that term, the entire class was reading rather well, Henry included.

I don't recall what salary that hard-working, organized teacher was paid. Perhaps it was five or ten dollars more per month than the previous teacher was paid, which was $40 per month. Both paid $10 per month for board and room in the farm home nearest the school.

For two of my middle-grade years I was taught by a tall, slim, male teacher who wore silver-rimmed glasses. He believed in not sparing the ruler across the knuckles and spoiling the child. He once kept Randy in at recess for some infraction of his rules, and the rest of us huddled under the window outside from where we could hear the whacks of the yardstick on Randy's bottom.

But this teacher had a redeeming quality; he could teach the subject matter well and motivated and inspired us to do our best. I especially enjoyed Friday afternoons when we got to try our hands at "industrial arts." We fashioned small pin trays from round pieces of metal that we cut from tin cans. We pounded these pieces into a depression in the end of a chunk of wood with a ball-peen hammer to give the metal a bowl shape. Then we made a smaller one, inverted it, and soldered it to the bottom of the larger piece. I made a huge Dutch girl lawn ornament and several other wooden items, too. My love of hammers, saws, files, sandpaper, brushes and paints started with his instruction. My various work projects won several ribbons at the county fair, and my puppet won a blue ribbon at the Minnesota State Fair.

Our school always put on a Christmas program of songs, plays and recitations, but I enjoyed the spring and fall Parents Visiting Day a little more. My mother always came, and the Schultz women (mother and daughter) came. They always enjoyed visiting, even though they had no one in school. I enjoyed reciting for the teacher in front of the visitors.

Winters in the '30's were cold and especially blustery. If there was new snow and much wind to cause drifting and a bad wind chill, Father would hitch a team of horses to our sleigh to take us to school or to come for us. Our close neighbors seemed to depend upon him to care for their children as well.

I remember with amazement the Svarthus family of four who had to walk three miles to get to school. They stayed home when it stormed, but on cold, sunny days they came walking past our place. They had no overshoes, and they always seemed to have large holes in the soles of their shoes. Their mother stuffed the shoes with thick, shiny paper from a catalog to cover the holes to keep out the snow. Each one wore a single pair of long cotton stockings and sometimes a pair of overalls, but their clothing was entirely inadequate. If they could not bear the elements any longer as they approached our driveway, they would turn in. They knew that Mother would shout at them to come into the house to warm themselves. She would remove their shoes and stockings and dry both the garments and their feet on the open oven door of our cookstove. There they sat with their feet propped up on warm bricks that Mother kept in the oven for that purpose.

While they were warming themselves, my sister and I got into our heavy snowpants and clumsy, four-buckle cloth overshoes, sweaters, scarves, and two pair of mittens. We could have walked to school, but my father took pity on the Svarthus children and hauled all of us to school by car. If the road was heavy with snow drifts, he hitched Prince and Dolly to the sleigh, and we had a comfortable ride huddled together in hay under a big horsehair robe.

Noon lunches were carried in a Karo syrup pail. Only a few had a store-bought lunch bucket. Everyone was poor, but some of us had a half-apple or an orange and cheese, jelly, or peanut butter sandwiches. Others, like the Svarthus children, had only coarse, home-made white bread spread with colorless margarine. They got lucky in times of desperation when their parents got on Relief (Welfare), for then they had grapefruit and celery and other strange food that I had never seen or tasted. I remember watching them with both pity and envy as they ate.

An older child was sent to pump fresh water from the well every morning. The school drinking fountain was rinsed out and filled with water. It was a five-gallon glass jug with a spigot at the bottom, but we all used the same drinking cup.

We experimented with hot lunches during the coldest period. Pupils brought macaroni, beans or meatballs in a small glass jar, and the teacher warmed these in a shallow pan of water over a kerosene burner. If the jar cracked from over-heating, one was simply out of luck.

Our school had central heating. The teacher built a fire in the basement furnace on the first cold morning and kept it going week after week all term, except for vacation periods, by banking the fire on Friday evenings and closing down the draft aperture. There would be enough glowing embers from the coal to get the fire going again Monday morning. Over the furnace was a huge, round grate in the floor. If one stood on the grate, one got red-faced and super-heated. If one stepped off, it was too cold for comfort, so the children fought for a tiny spot on the grate. When the wind blew excessively and when it was sub-zero in temperature, we kept our coats and overshoes on, often tapping the floor with our toes to improve circulation while we studied.

At the peak of enrollment in District 45 there were 47 students. This was a very big job for one teacher, but we had a capable person teaching at that time. She would call out for one class to come to the front of the room, saying "second grade reading" or "fourth grade arithmetic." That class would sit in a semi-circle on small chairs. They would have eight to ten minutes to hand in their papers and get assignments with the teacher's explanations. Then the next class would come forward.

With so many pupils of all ages we were hard to beat in Field Day activities in the spring. We competed against one or two other districts. I was poor at softball, but with my long legs I was able to win a ribbon or two for running and relays. I also enjoyed sack races and the three-legged race.

Another spring activity centered around the striped gophers awakening from hibernation. Their holes were everywhere on the school grounds and in the fields and pastures. The township paid a small bounty for dead gophers which the catcher had to prove by presenting the tails to a township officer. The favorite recess and after-school activity became the pursuit of the gopher. Usually a girl would pump a pail full of water from the school well and pour it slowly down a gopher hole while a boy would stand over the other end of the runway with a ready baseball bat held high. Some gophers would come hurtling out in all possible haste and sometimes escaped, but the gopher who hesitated got knocked out of existence in a second. Then the boy would cut off the tail with a pocket knife. Each gopher tail would bring three cents in bounty.

Ernie, our seven-year old neighbor boy, brought his collection of tails to our house because my father was a township supervisor. Only Mother was at home. Ernie announced that he had tails as he walked into the dining room and started to empty a tall K.C. Baking Powder can onto the dining room table! Before my mother could react, there was a pile of smelly, rotting tails on the table corner, a few dribbling onto the floor. "Fisssh!" Ernie said as he wrinkled up his nose. He had a twinkle in his eyes and a proud grin on his face.

He had, indeed, been diligent in eradicating gophers. Mother counted them hastily as she dropped each tail back into the tall can. She counted out $1.26, a lot of pocket money for a seven-year old boy in those days. Then she took the tails and dumped them in the outdoor toilet where they could not be retrieved. With his can in his hand and money in his pocket, Ernie churned his little legs homeward.

There were P.T.A. (Parent-Teacher Association) meetings each month throughout the term, always held during the evening. The children came with the parents. After the business portion of the meeting a program of entertainment could be counted on. I tapdanced to three melodies played on the piano by my teacher and tap instructor at one such meeting. Once a year a basket social was held, usually to raise money for a special project.

One spring P.T.A. business meeting turned into a brawl. A bachelor farmer was especially vocal in protesting the proposed district payment for graduates to ride the school bus to town to attend high school in the fall. He shook his fist at the crowd and pounded on the podium with white knuckles as he ranted. His brother, father of three, loudly protested a smallpox vaccination program that was being encouraged by the county office of education. After a lenghty free-for-all of noisy opinion-giving, one father, named Martin, stood up and demanded the floor and told the others to be quiet. They obeyed him because he had not been one of the argumentative ones hereto. He turned to that protesting father of three and asked, "Al, did you vaccinate your hogs this year?"

"Of course I did!" was the hasty reply.

Martin's second question followed before the man realized what was happening:

"Do you mean to tell me you vaccinated your hogs to protect them from cholera, but that you won't vaccinate your children to protect them from smallpox?"

A rumble of murmuring ran through the crowd while a couple of fellows cheered, a vote was taken, and we did get our vaccinations. It was also decided to support the school bus and that each family would pay $2 per month per student to ride the bus to get to high school in Battle Lake.

Change was strenuously resisted by some stubborn older folk and by some who were childless. One father refused to let his son be the first in his family to attend high school. The son, however, was so determined to go that he walked the seven-and-a-half miles to town each day until the father finally gave in. I hope that he was proud when his son much later earned a college degree!

Finally, the most longed-for day came when school was dismissed for summer vacation, and children and parents alike celebrated with a big school picnic. We had a softball-playing, rope-jumping, relay-racing day on the shores of Ottertail Lake or Round Lake. It was a day for hot dogs and icecream cones, potluck lunch and all the real lemonade thirsty, growing children could consume. The lemonade was made up in clean, new cream cans. Even the non-parents in the community joined in the fun. I know that I always went home emotionally refreshed, physically tired, and usually sunburned. I had gotten much more from the term than the three R's.

Bidding for a Basket

Bake sales seem to be a primary source of income for small groups these days, but in the 1930's and '40's, it was the basket social. People no longer seem to have as much fun when they try putting on a basket social now. I think the big difference is that it used to involve the entire family and community, the elderly and the youths included. Everyone would also put some heart into it!

When a PTA, church group or 4-H club held a basket social, some very creative and elaborate baskets showed up. These were usually large decorated shoeboxes or other large containers that could hold a huge lunch for two. They were most often decorated with many yards of colorful,crimped crepe paper and bows and sometimes cupie dolls or figurines.

Prizes were given for the most creative or loveliest boxes.

Because the creators of the boxes were kept secret before the sale, the prizes were pinned on the box in the form of a blue or special ribbon, or even a dollar bill. Winning boxes were held up for applause.

Sometimes there would be elaborate designs such as a big red barn with Gothic roof, windows, Dutch doors, and a silo concealing a thermos bottle filled with hot chocolate. Once I saw a basket lunch put up in an old wicker fishing tackle box. Someone made a basket like a white rural church with a steeple and stained glass windows. There were also baskets like rural schoolhouses or bird houses for martins.

The lazy gals took the easy way out by creating a hobo lunch in a red hankie tied to a husky stick. Most boxes, though, were feminine creations using ruffles, lace and bows.

There was always an auctioneer, real or self-made, in the community who could put on a funny performance selling the baskets to the male buyers huddled on one side of the room. The ladies and girls would wait on the other side, giggling and blushing in anticipation. They had gone to great lengths to get their baskets there concealed so that peeking eyes would not see their baskets before the sale.

The baskets were usually delivered wrapped in newspaper or a burlap bag or sent in via another woman. The name of the creator of the box was hidden somewhere on the outside, but the creator usually came forward as soon as the buyer had retired to a seat. If there were too many baskets, some men bought two.

It happened that a girl would let her sweetheart peek at her basket so he'd be sure to buy hers. When the bidding started, that young man would invariably bid so eagerly that the other bidders caught onto whose basket it was. Then they would bid up that basket to where the poor man would have to decide whether to pay an outrageous price or to stop bidding. If he was clever, he would suddenly stop at the right point to make the insincere bidder pay the outrageous price.

It was not uncommon for two young bucks to battle it out bidding over a certain girl's basket, either. At such times the girl would end up eating lunch with the community's most obnoxious bachelor. Sweethearts are known to have broken up over basket socials.

The other side of the coin was that a fellow could get a certain girl's attention by succeeding in buying her basket, and so it happened that some couples met and started dating after the basket social.

Children would have fun guessing whose basket was being sold and taking verbal bets on who the successful bidder would be. Small children sometimes accompanied the mother so she'd have to have packed enough lunch for them, too.

The food consisted of hearty sandwiches, sometimes baked chicken drumsticks, a piece of cake or pie for each, fruit and candy. Certain married women had a reputation for making super-fine lunches, a few others for tasteless, dull lunches, so the married man also tried to find out whose basket to bid on, not necessarily his wife's.

When the bidding was over, one could see young gals eating with old grandpas, sweethearts torn asunder or eating together as they had hoped, and women eating with their neighbor's husband or hired man. Most were not disappointed with their food and all had a good time. Laughter and the chatter of conversation filled the room.

Basket socials netted more money than bake sales. I remember one basket in the 1940's selling for as high as $20. Most went for $2 or $3, but a few sold for $5. People didn't have as many kinds of entertainment that required money then, and therefore they were more generous in bidding for a good cause. There was also the occasional show-off who spent most of his entire month's wages to impress a certain girl.

Most people then would have told you it was the night of family and community fun–not the money generated–that made basket socials a hit.

Hans

Early every December our rural teachers handed out Christmas seals to each pupil to sell to our parents and neighbors without children in school. The money went to fight tuberculosis which was still a threat to some families and individuals. It was diminishing, but we knew of a few persons being treated for the disease. Treatment was usually a stay of several weeks or months in a sanitorium, a dormitory where the patient got a good diet, lots of bed rest, and plenty of clean, fresh air.

It was not easy selling any worthwhile amount of Christmas

seals. People in the early 1930's had no money to spare. Some households bought a dime's worth which was ten seals. Some bought a nickel's worth, and some could buy nothing. A very few donated 15 or 20 cents.

When school let out, I cut diagonally across the fields with my sister as fast as our legs could carry us to be the first to get to the Schultz home. Mrs. Schultz and her single daughter, an adult, would be willing to buy 15 or 20 cents worth. We usually got a cookie there, as well, to encourage us to hurry on to sell to someone else. It was fun to go there because no one made us feel more welcome or useful in our mission.

The Schultzes also had an adult son, Hans. He had been crippled from birth, as far as I know. He was very thin, and he stooped forward and walked erratically. His speech was difficult to understand, and he drooled. But he was intelligent and had finished high school. Hans seldom came to any community social event, but he came to our farm on an occasional errand. Mother always invited him in for lunch and treated him with respect.

One day Hans came into our yard simply to walk through enroute to another neighbor. We had an electric fence to hold in our cattle from the grainfields. My father watched with amazement as Hans crawled slowly through the fence, holding the wire in his hands. Father told him to wait a bit while he went to turn off the battery, but Hans waved away the offer and climbed through. The ground was damp from recent rain, but the shocks didn't seem to bother Hans. He climbed through the electric fence coming back, too, and he didn't seem to feel the shocks at all.

One crisp April morning as I was walking to school with several companions, I observed Hans walking with his little dog, a tiny, nondescript mutt, to the mailbox beside the main road. He had to cross the main road to reach the box, and the dog crossed right behind him. Just as they turned to recross the road after mailing a letter, a big car came careening down the slope without slowing down in the least. Hans scurried out of the way with his dog a couple steps behind him. The driver swerved, quite deliberately, toward the dog, hitting it and then tearing up the next hill at breakneck speed. We children were horror-struck at such deliberate cruelty! We recognized the driver as a relative of our teacher.

Hans dropped to his knees, crying out to his motionless dog. He stooped and gently and agonizingly picked up his lifeless companion, got to his feet somehow and staggered homeward with his burden. Hans had lost the only true friend and pal he had in the world. The only creature who accepted him and loved him the way he was.

Such cruelty to a fellow human being and to an animal most of us had never witnessed. We children angrily and tearfully hurried to school and hung up our outer wraps in the cloakroom and went to claim a spot over the furnace register. We discussed the horrid experience quite loudly to make sure that our teacher heard the whole story. I hated that man as long as I knew him.

The Schultz family had built a new, long chicken house many years earlier. Before they had a chance to use it for chickens, their home burned to the ground. Few things were saved, and they could not afford to build a new house, so they moved into the chicken house to live temporarily. The Depression came, and the lack of funds made it a permanent home.

The coziness of their humble home was matched by their warm personalities. Whenever our cattle dog, Sport, became terrified of lightning and thunder and no one was home to let him in, he tore past other neighbors straight to the Schultz door, and they gave him shelter and soothing words. Several times Sport was missing when we came home in the rain and thunderstorms. We always found him in their care.

Hans's sister, Marie, later married our bachelor-farmer neighbor, Sam. Sam had come to America from Denmark with two companions as a young man, only to get drafted and sent back to Europe to fight World War I. They eventually returned and became farmers in our area.

The Schultz parents died in turn, then Hans in his middle years. Marie was very ill and hospitalized when her brother died and could not possibly make the arrangements or attend the funeral. Sam was not up to it, so Mike did it all. Mike was another member of the trio from Denmark.

Mike danced to a different drummer. He was intelligent and a good talker, but he had the original hippie look regarding clothing and hairstyle. His hair just grew and grew and grew. His shirt and overall and other clothing was worn night and day, week in, week out, month in, month out. Every summer he took a lengthy bath in the lake near Sam's place, wearing all his soiled clothes while he bathed. Then he went into the dense woods and stripped and hung the wet garments on the fence to dry and put on a clean set of clothes.

But when he was needed to make arrangements for Hans's

funeral, he took a bath, went to Battle Lake for a haircut and a shave, and drove to Fergus Falls where he bought new clothing.

Mike took care of everything and came to the funeral clean shaven and baby clean. He looked downright handsome in his new dressy suit and white shirt and tie. He told Mother, who complimented him on his looks, that he even had new underwear, socks and shoes. Hans got a proper burial, and Marie was very pleased to hear how it all turned out.

It must have felt good, because Mike stayed clean and neat after that. Marie was there for Mike's burial when his time came. Sam had died earlier, and Marie lived alone for some years. During this time she and I exchanged several letters and cards, and I went to see her now and then.

They are all gone away to their reward now. I learned some real values by the example of these friendly, caring folk.

Sport

Most farmers as well as city dwellers during the '20's and '30's could not afford to feed a litter of puppies, so they were given away, destroyed or abandoned if they could not be sold. So it was no real surprise when my parents came home from a trip to town and found a puppy about two months old sitting on their front porch steps. They had heard of other abandoned puppies.

They inquired of the neighbors and made it known in town and everywhere they went that a stray pup had been found at our home. No one came to claim him, so they kept him and raised him on table scraps and milk from the cows. The table scraps consisted mostly of boiled potatoes and a little gravy or fat drippings, a diet not beginning to measure up to present-day puppy formulas.

They named him Sport, not a very original name as male dogs at that time were usually given the name Sport, Shep or Rover.

The well-rounded pup looked rather ordinary, but as he matured it was the opinion of many onlookers that he was of good breeding. He was a wavy-haired white pup with black ears and had large black spots on the body. He had rather long, wavy fur that grew thick in winter, making him seem larger than the medium-sized dog that he was.

I was not yet born when Sport came to our home. My sister, who was nearly two years old, became the dog's constant pal. Then I was born and that first summer when I was placed on the lawn to sit or crawl, Sport guarded me by chasing chickens and geese away that ventured too close. He was not an angry dog, but he would have killed to protect my sister or me.

Sport got no training from my parents because they knew nearly nothing about training a dog. But he got lots of love. He was not yet a year old when he showed his own good breeding by chasing our cow herd from the rear like a proper dog. He never barked at them at the head. Before long my father could say, "Sport, get the cows!", and Sport would head for the pasture and in minutes would bring the small herd home at a brisk walk, never on the run. A mutual respect developed between the dog and the cows so that they started for home when they saw him coming at a distance.

Before long Sport learned to take the big metal hook in his mouth and unhook the Dutch door of the barn, then jump on the door to push it open. It was too tight to close, but the fact that he could open the door saved my father some steps.

Some pigs got out of their pen one hot afternoon. Anyone who has ever tried to catch a pig on the loose knows what a problem they can be. They are equally impossible to herd, so chasing them back into the pen was out of the question. Sport observed my father diving to the ground as he tried to grab them by the legs, so he ran up to one pig and took an ear between his teeth. The pig stopped and stood as if glued to the ground. Father came and put a rope around the pig and got him wrestled into the pen while Sport captured another one. It was all instinctive. Sport saved my father a lot of hard work that day and got a lot of loving praise in return.

Sport was also a good hunting dog. Whenever Father shot mallards in our slough, Sport swam out and retrieved them.

As soon as Sport observed sharp lightning or heard loud thunder, he would dash for the kitchen door and beg to come in. When the door was opened, he would head for his security spot under the kitchen table and would stay there until the storm was over. He was never a house dog at any other time. If lightning or thunder occurred when no one was home, he would set out for his friends, the Schultzes, a little over half a mile away. Early in his life he had apparently tried our closest neighbors without getting invited in, so when he was let in at the Schultz home, he never forgot their hospitality. Even though they fed him and petted him, he never left home to go there for any other reason than a storm. Sport always stayed on our yard unless ordered to go to the pasture or a field.

During the last two years of his life Sport's hearing began to fail. His eyesight may have failed some as well. My father backed the car out from the garage and ran over Sport with one back wheel. Sport had a sore front leg for awhile. Then the cream hauler ran over Sport with both the front and back wheels of the cream truck because Sport neither saw nor heard him coming. I could only watch in horror, and the driver felt terrible about it; but Sport seemed no worse for the experience. He neither limped nor showed any signs of pain.

As the months rolled by, he began to sleep most of the day as well as at night. He looked old. When his appetite also failed him, we realized that the end was not far away. My father wanted to shoot him because he could not bear to see him waste away, but my sister would not hear of that. She was only a couple of years older than the dog and had grown up with him. So the situation continued until the dog was obviously not going to live more than a few days. My father was an expert at putting down sick horses and dogs, so at last he shot and buried the dog that he loved. When my sister came home from school and learned what had happened, she cried for days. I cried, too, but I felt as my father felt that this was the humane and kinder way for our dear friend. In fact the whole neighborhood missed Sport because he was legendary.

I am thankful that God sent us that rare and wonderful pup. We never found out from where he had come, but someone else's compassion for the pup in not wanting to destroy him was their loss and our gain. Despite his meager diet he was a healthy dog. He was never wormed, never given a shot, never given a vitamin pill, food supplement, or commercial dog food, and he was never ill or in need of a veterinarian's care. Sport, the Wonder Dog, lived with us for a full sixteen years.

My Father's Son

My father had no sons, so he needed my help quite often to hold up the two sides of the cotton Bemis bags while he scooped up oats from our granary floor to fill them. Then he would lift the hefty sack up and bang it on the floor three or four times to settle the grain, leaving room for another scoop of grain on top. He would then tie the end of the sack with twine by making three twists around and pull up a loop so hard that it would stay "tied" without an actual knot.

The bags were loaded onto our wagon and hauled to town, pulled by our car, seven miles into Battle Lake to the elevator. There I enjoyed watching as Father untied each bag with a jerk of the end of the twine and dumped the grain onto the grates in the elevator floor. A little later the ground grain was sacked up under a spout, tied again, and hauled home for turkey feed. He bought bags of specially prepared turkey concentrate to mix with the ground oats.

For me there was a lot of sitting in the car, waiting. I watched the chirping house sparrows and other small birds gleaning the spilled grain in and near the elevator. Sometimes a neighbor would pull up and wave at me. A trip to town gave Father a chance to visit with other farmers, so the waiting sometimes seemed endless.

Another job that I regularly helped Father do was to sharpen sickle blades on our round grindstone mounted on an axle. I don't know who invented it, but all Norwegians seemed to own one. It had a tiny metal seat behind the stone where Father sat while he pedaled the mechanism to make the stone go around quite rapidly. He held the sickle blade against the stone at the proper angle, and it was my job to pour a trickle of water on the point of contact to cool it and prevent sparks. It seemed to sharpen better with the use of water, too. Sometimes we also sharpened the big blade of the scythe in this manner. I learned to use the scythe at an early age, but Mother was the one who could really swing the scythe in cutting weeds.

Corn wasn't combined in those days. It was either cut up for the silo or it was cut and tied into bundles, brought home and picked by hand. That is called corn husking. The stalk and leaves were thrown to the cattle for feed. Father taught me to husk corn, but it was rough work, murder on the hands. I could manage to get enough corn husked to feed a pig or two and to get enough to feed the hand-operated corn sheller to get a pail of corn for my adult ducks. I lost a lot of fingernails husking corn.

Horses provided the power for my father's farmwork. They moved the brooder houses and plowed the fields. They pulled the hay wagons and cultivated the corn.

We usually had mixed breeds, but I remember one sorrel Belgian mare and one dapple-grey Percheron gelding, both heavy-weights with big feet. I was afraid to get near them because of those huge feet unless they were tied in their stalls. It took a strong man just to carry their heavy leather harnesses and to sling them onto their tall backs. In hot weather we also covered the harness with a fly net made of leather strings sewed together at one end. These had leather fringes that flopped along the horses's sides as they walked, repelling the flies.

I was a young teenager when one day I brought lunch to my father in the field. He asked me to bring the team home to the barn because he wanted to stay in the field and shock the grain bundles that lay scattered in rows. I had never done this and was apprehensive but eager to be handed the reins to four horses.

We had not gotten far when I understood that Father knew what he was doing in giving me that job; the big four-horse team were so eager to get back to the barn for water and hay that they literally pulled me across those 40 acres of field, heading straight for the barn. I did not have the strength to hold them back or to steer them, but they knew where to go and took me home. I managed to unhook them from each other and get them into the barn with their harnesses on. They each knew which stall to go to.

Father got a small Allis Chalmers C tractor about a year before we moved off our farm. I was soon 17, and he tried to teach me to drive it pulling our grain binder–the machine that cut the ripe grain and tied it into bundles. I could not make the corners square enough to suit him, so he drove the tractor while I sat on the binder to trip the bundles at the proper time. That did not please him, either, because some of the bundles got too fat, some too thin. It was tough trying to be my father's son! Lucky for me that I didn't do very well; he never asked me to try it again.

I carried wood in for our cookstove daily when I grew big enough to handle the job. I didn't like the weight of the heavy oak wood.

I had some indoor work, too. Now and then I had to sit

beside the wooden butter churn and crank the handle. The minutes dragged by as I turned and listened to the sloshing cream get heavier and thicker. The job I truly hated the most was to wash the cream separator. Hot water cooled off too fast and became greasy to the touch. I especially hated washing the 34 individual metal, cone-shaped disks from the mechanism that separates the cream from the milk.

A cream separator puts the cream into one pail, the milk into another. Carl Gustaf de Laval of Sweden invented it in 1877, and the De Laval separator was the main type used in the 1930's. It had a big, round holding tank and a rotating bowl-shaped container full of metal disks and a spout for cream and a spout for milk. A hand crank turned the rotating bowl. A gasoline motor could also be used, but that tended to go too fast.

The whole milk from the cow was poured into the holding tank, and it had a spigot that let the milk drain very slowly into the bowl under it. This bowl rotated rapidly, and the centrifugal force caused by the rotation sent the lighter cream toward the center and the heavier ingredients to the outer wall of the bowl.

A fatty substance full of dirt and impurities collected at the base of these disks, around the inner edge of the bowl. It had the consistency of petroleum jelly. Dirty Vaseline. I had to remove a strip of it an inch wide with my fingers and put it into the garbage sack before washing the bowl, the disks, and the spouts in soapy, hot water. Then rinse and wipe them. This washing was done every forenoon, and the cows had to be milked again in the evening, so it was usually done again, at least in warm weather. It was a never-ending, thankless task.

Sometimes I was glad that Father frequently had me helping him outdoors so that my sister had to wash the separator–until she left home.

I became somewhat of a tomboy, but I also learned to sew and to crochet, thanks to my talented mother who taught us what she knew how to do. She was also a good gardener and passed that skill on to us as well.

It had been a miserably hot day in August, and Father was working with a threshing crew on a neighbor's farm. I truly looked forward to a Saturday evening in Battle Lake where I always met a friend or more and occasionally took in a movie, now that I was sixteen.

Bathrooms did not exist in farm homes in my neighborhood, so I had taken a cold water bath in a big, galvanized tub out in our pump house. I had brought out a big teakettle full of hot water to take the chill off the cold well water. We took our baths in the farm kitchen during winter, but doing it in the pump house during hot weather saved having to clean up. All that was necessary was to rinse out the tub and pour the water on the ground.

I had gone back to the house to get into fresh clothing, a paisley print dirndl skirt and a white peasant blouse. With my new sandals on, all that was left to do was to comb my hair. Why wasn't Father home yet? I would possibly miss the movie if he were late. Mother was also getting ready to go to town.

The telephone rang, and Mother answered. Father wanted to talk to me. The threshing rig had somehow broken down and had gotten repaired, he said, but he had to stay and help unload four wagonloads of bundles, just in case it should rain. He would be very late. I was to go to the pasture and bring home the cows and start milking.

My jaw dropped. One did not argue with a parent in those days about something so logical and necessary. It was with a painful, protesting spirit that I undressed and put on my grubby work clothes. I knew there would be no trip to town, no movie, no friends until next Saturday night, if then. My bathing had been for nothing.

I shed angry tears as I walked nearly a mile to find the cattle. I was already hot and sweaty when I got them into the barn. My sister was going to school in Minneapolis, or I would make her help, I thought. But she had usually done housework, and I was the son Father never had. Mother had never taken a hand with the milking, and suddenly I realized how wise she was.

Eight cows. All big Holsteins. Some had huge teats; one or two had short nubbins. I had often helped during summer, but I had never milked over two cows in one sitting. I pulled up the milk stool beside the cow in the first stall. Squirt, squirt, right hand, left hand, in a steady rhythm. It went easily and rapidly. She milked about ten or eleven quarts. On to the next cow. This was one with tight, short nubbins. Besides that, she kicked at flies constantly. Her tail banged my clean hair just twice before I gave up on her and moved to the third cow. I would leave her until last, hoping Father would get home to milk her.

Things were going along fine, but my hands and arms were getting trembly and weak, even painful, with all this squeezing motion. I had a hard time finishing that cow.

The fourth cow had huge teats that were easy to hang on to, but she had sores on them and tried to hold her milk. I had to dip my hands into the milk to wet her teats to ease the pain on her tender spots. After much squeezing, she grew weary of holding it back and began to relax. It would have gone along just fine if only my arm muscles could have held up. My weak, trembling arms and hands were matched only by my now-screaming lower back.

I had skipped the second cow and milked only four and was soon done with another cow when Father walked into the barn. He was grateful for my efforts and he took over, finishing the one I was working on. I knew that I would never have managed to milk all eight.

I was too tired to take a full bath again, so I washed my hands and my limbs and called it a day. The bed was the only place for my tired and sore muscles, and I soon floated off to Battle Lake in my dreams. I was a sorry substitute for a son.

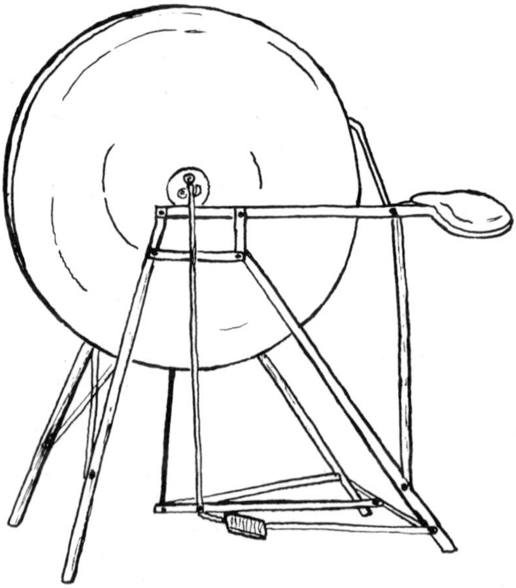

The Grindstone

Checking Corn

A few farm-raised adults can still remember fields of checked corn. The hills of corn were spaced three feet apart in each row, and the rows were three feet apart, forming a perfect checkerboard pattern. The planting of corn in this manner was called checking corn, and it was used generally until farmers began to use large tractors and plant larger fields. The farmer who checked his corn very accurately could cultivate it from east to west and again from north to south. Three such cross cultivations kept it weed-free, and chemicals were not used.

The two-horse, two-row corn planter had two round metal containers that held the seed corn. A roll of wound up sturdy wire was brought to the field on the back of the planter. This roll was roughly 20 inches in diameter, and the wire had knots in it every three feet. One end of this wire was staked at the start of the row, and it was unrolled by the planter as the planter was driven to the opposite end of the field. Here the roll was removed from the planter and the end of the wire was again staked to the ground.

The farmer then turned the corn planter around and attached the wire into the trip gadget off to one side. This trip mechanism rotated a seeding plate at the bottom of the seed boxes. Each time a knot in the wire tripped the gadget, three seeds fell through the seed plate, down into a tube that ended in a planter shoe where the seed was deposited into the soil. The wheels of the planter covered the seeds with soil.

Each row was planted in the same manner. The wire had to be moved for each row. The tension of the wire had to be kept exactly the same over the whole field so the seed would be planted exactly three feet apart. The work was made more difficult in hilly or rough terrain.

Checked corn got more sunlight exposure than drilled corn and had a larger area for its roots to draw moisture. The ears grew larger than on drilled corn and produced more per acre. Less seed was required to check corn. The obvious benefit over present day methods is the non-use of chemicals for weed control.

All corn and other crops were fertilized by barnyard manure. Crops were rotated to prevent loss of a particular nutrient in the soil. Sweet clover, Sudan grass and other crops could be plowed under as "green manure" to build up the soil. It was a chemical-free way of farming.

It was fun to play hide-and-seek in these cornfields. A child could run in any direction unhindered by a solid wall of cornstalks as we have in today's drilled corn row. A field of checked corn was a beautiful sight as the rows looked perfect from any side of the field. Even looking at the field diagonally, the rows were perfect.

I think this was farming as God intended it.

Surviving the 1940 Blizzard

The terrible November 11th storm of 1940, better known as the Armistice Day Blizzard, was the worst storm in anyone's memory where I lived. It struck very suddenly in mid-to-late afternoon with dropping temperatures, heavy snow and strong wind. Lightly clad hunters, shoppers and travelers across the state were caught away from home and soon found themselves on blocked roads or unable to find their way on foot. Many perished in the storm.

The raging white-out kept our family isolated in our home for over two days and nights. Our house and barn were only 100 feet apart, but the dark red barn was not visible from the house even momentarily in the swirling snow those days as the wind raged. It was so bad my father risked his life each time he went to the barn to hand-milk the cows and feed and water the animals. Had he lost his sense of direction, he would have perished.

Father found ropes in our basement and tied them together. He tied one end to our porch cornerpost, the other to a heavy chunk of wood from the woodbox. With the chunk of wood in hand, he set out in the direction of the barn. I remember seeing his dark, bending form disappearing in the storm.

When father got close enough to glimpse the red barn in the swirling snow, he was out of rope length. He pushed the chunk end-down into the snow so he could find it again after doing the chores for the return trip to the house.

The storm began to subside during the early hours of the third morning, and my father discovered that our adult

Narragansett turkeys, intended for market that week, had started to roost in the lower branches of the trees in our yard when the storm struck. There all who roosted still clung, frozen to the tree limbs, dead.

At noon we discovered dime-sized steam vents in the hard snowdrifts. Father dug into such a vent and found a turkey, cold and barely alive.

Mother and I came out to help, but first I waded through deep drifts to check on my ducks. My four adult Pekin ducks were fine in their log shed. They had clean, dry straw to lie on, but only ice in their water pail. They had eaten snow from the tiny drifts that formed by the door. They were out of food. I tended to their needs at once.

For two days we dug turkeys out of the drifts and managed to save many of them by carrying them into the barn, placing them on dry straw in front of the cattle mangers. It was relatively warm in the barn filled with cattle and horses. By placing the stiff turkeys side by side, their small amount of body heat mingled with another's body heat. I seem to recall that we saved about a fourth of the 250 to 300 turkeys in the flock.

Part of the following day was spent yanking the roosting dead birds from the tree branches with garden rakes.

Mindy and Cats with Narragansett Turkeys

Toward the end of the third day Father decided to break into the huge drift that covered much of the corn crib and the entire lean-to behind it. This was the home of our butchering hog who we were sure had perished there.

Suddenly I noticed a tiny hole with a trace of water vapor coming from it. "Father, look!" I said. "It's just like the turkeys–a hole in the drift!"

Hope returned. Father dug diligently as the drift was hard and deep. At last he fell through the drift and there, beside his feet, was our pig. To our utter amazement, it was not only alive but almost cozy. It had eaten all its food and licked snow, forming a tiny cave around itself. It was truly happy to see us but happier still to get food and water.

We had learned much about survival for ourselves and our animals; much about hope and resourcefulness.

A few months later, on March 15, 1941, we were tested again by another bad two-day blizzard. It was quite a winter!

Riding the School Bus

The yellow school bus that took me into Battle Lake when I started high school in 1943 had traveled for over one hour when it reached the corner where I got on. The entire bus route was 54 miles long, and I lived seven miles from the end of the route. That meant when I got on late in the morning, I had to ride for an hour and a half after school.

To be fair to all, the route was reversed every week. Then I got on at 7:10 a.m. and rode the remaining 47 miles of the route before getting to school. But I had the joy of getting home within a half hour after school let out.

Meeting the bus at 7:10 a.m. during the shortened days of winter was very unpleasant for me because I had to walk a half mile in moonlight or pitch darkness, and I had to wait, unsheltered, at the corner with my friend, DeLoris. We often stood there, stomping our feet to try keeping them warm. Sometimes the wait stretched to ten minutes, sometimes a half hour, depending on road conditions. A few times we stood there over an hour before giving up and going home to find out later the bus had been stuck and school had closed.

We dressed warmly out of neccessity. At 10 or 20 degrees below zero, we didn't argue with our mothers who tied a wool scarf around our faces, covering mouth and nose, and another scarf around the forehead. But when we saw the school bus approaching, we were quick to yank off our scarves.

We wore wool slacks over colored cotton tights under our skirts, and we removed the slacks when we got to school. Leather snow boots, fleece lined and laced up, became popular for a short time.

Spring school days and early fall days could make for a hot, dusty ride over the gravel roads. Restlessness and boredom became a problem on the long bus ride. We dared not misbehave because the drivers had a policy of stopping the bus to wait for order to be restored. None of us wanted to delay getting home, so we usually got quiet as soon as we felt the bus slowing down.

One girl, Dorothy, hated a certain timid boy on the bus. In fact, none of the girls liked him in the least. Dorothy carried a small purse and she had her box of face powder with her. Knowing this, another boy, Robert, grabbed her purse, took out her powder puff and rubbed it on the detested boy's face before throwing it back to her. She grumbled and threatened Robert but did nothing about it. It was forgotten until the route was almost completed. Only four of us remained on the bus, and Robert was sitting in the front seat. Dorothy got up and walked forward to get off the bus at her driveway, prepared for sweet revenge. As she passed Robert and was about to step down the three steps, her right hand emptied her whole powder box on top of Robert's short Heinie haircut. Powder dribbled down his neck and onto his ears and shoulders, and he choked in a cloud of fine dust. By the time he realized what had happened, she was gone and the bus was rolling. That was one time the stern driver laughed heartily. Robert left Dorothy alone after that.

My Hero

Many men came to work for my father on our farm at various times, but we seldom had more than one hired man at a time. They came to live with us, sleeping in our house and eating at our table, and Mother did their laundry. Some we liked, and some we were glad to dismiss as soon as a particular job was done. Two are especially memorable for various reasons.

Ole was a middle-aged bachelor with a heavy Norwegian accent. When he used our telephone, a wooden box with a mouthpiece and a crank, he rang a long ring to which the operator responded with, "Number please." Ole always called home and only home, so he always answered, "Two four," more like "Tooooooo foooooor" with a long, deadpan drawl. Thus he came to be known as Two Four in our household, but that was never used in his presence.

Two Four was very dependable and honest, two reasons why we kept him on for longer periods of time than most. He was also a kind and good-natured man, and he seemed to enjoy teasing me, a child of 8-10 years. When I did something cute, naughty, or rather stupid, he would say in Norwegian, "*Du er ikke verd salt i maten!*" This translated is "You are not worth the salt in your food!" This was usually accompanied by a slap with the back of his hand on my behind.

One summer Saturday evening found our family in Battle Lake for groceries and an evening of visiting with friends and neighbors on the sidewalk. Two Four came along, and just as we piled into the car to go home, he decided to return to the grocery store to buy candy bars as a treat for us girls. (Donna, a cousin from Minneapolis, was also with us that evening.) Mother started to protest because she knew how very little money he had, but he went anyway.

Two Four returned with his purchase and handed each of us two bars as we drove homeward. He was sitting in the front seat beside my mother, with Father driving, and we girls sat in the back seat. We thanked him and opened a bar each and took a bite. *Uff da!* Such an awful bitter molasses taste! Medicinal! In the moonlight we read the wrappers. It was not candy but some kind of supplementary vitamin health bars. We were not fussy about the kind of candy bars we ate, but this was worse than trying to convince ourselves that Ex-lax is fully as delicious as a Hershey bar. We quickly wrapped up the remainder and pocketed it until we got home. While Mother unlocked the house door, we three girls dashed for the little house with the half-moon in the door (outdoor toilet) almost bursting with giggles. There, at the base of an ash tree, grew some brush out of a pile of machine parts and junk. We kept the wrappers but threw the bars into this clump of brush.

The next day at the dinner table I, full of spunk, began to make remarks about the leaf lettuce being served having lots of vitamins. We three girls got an instant case of giggles that we could not turn off. I felt a hot jab in my shinbone from Mother's shoe, but I was unable to stop giggling, though I tried hard. Donna remarked how well the brush was growing in the junk pile and I just HAD to say, "It must be the vitamins." I got another swift jab from Mother's shoe, and I had to leave the table.

I liked Two Four because he was a cat lover as I am. I remember him fondly aiming a squirt of milk from the cow's teat into an eager cat's mouth until the cat was satisfied. Less clever cats got their portion in a dish.

My favorite hired man was about twelve years older than I. When he first came to work, I was just eight years old and was a genuine pest, merciless in seeking his attention. He enjoyed me and hated me by turns. He was a rather nervous, tall, wiry man with a warm personality, and he liked kids. Father liked him because he was a dependable and capable worker.

Ernest milked the cows by hand while the flies bit both man and beast, and the cows swished their urine-soaked tails from side to side over his head to remove the biting flies. I pestered him while he worked until he'd drop the milk stool, dump the milk into the separator, and run after me with the intention of spanking me. But I was slim and fleet of foot and managed to spring into a narrow horse manger to lie face up, kicking my feet into the air so he couldn't spank.

I pestered Ernest with cigarette butts when he was trying to quit smoking. I made myself such a pest that he once literally buried me under a huge pitchfork load of hay that he was carrying into the barn. Before I got out from under it, he caught me, and then I got a spanking.

Getting even became my passion. I stood behind the pump house beside the milk cooler which was a deep, concrete tank filled with very cold well water. I held a tall KC Baking Powder can full of cold water, and when Ernest came around the corner with milk cans to rinse out, I threw the cold water, hitting him in the chest. Then I fled before he could get his breath back.

The next day I came around that same corner for water for my ducklings just as he was rinsing milk foam from the inside of the tall cans. He let fly with about two gallons of foamy milk-water, and I walked right into this shower intended for me. The cold water on this very hot day took my breath away as I turned and ran to the house basement, hair and clothing thoroughly drenched. Milk foam can feel very sticky, and we had no running water or bathroom. I put a galvanized tub on the basement floor beside the drain and peeled off my soggy clothes for a cold water shampoo and bath. I had learned that one lesson the hard way.

Ernest and my sister were told to weed the garden one July 4th before going to town in the evening for the festivities. My sister may have been fifteen then, and I trailed by three and a half years. I was told to help, but I did more pestering than weeding, always managing to get into Ernest's way. He had a cap gun in his hind pocket that he had won at a carnival the night before. At last in frustration he pulled out the gun and a roll of caps and showed me how to load it. Then he gave it to me on the promise that I get out of the garden and stay out. I did. I still have the cap gun, and it still works.

Along came World War II, and my carefree life suddenly took a serious turn. Ernest was drafted. My sister and I wrote bi-monthly letters to him, and he enjoyed hearing about the farm activities and the animals. He was sent to Africa to fight Rommel, the Desert Fox. During heavy fighting at Fondouk, Ernest was hit by a German machine gun bullet that went through his left shoulder, breaking up a rib and collapsing a lung. Two fellow soldiers helped him to retreat on foot about a half-mile behind enemy lines. There they laid him beside a clump of cactus and dusted sulfa powder on his wounds to stop the bleeding. They left him there alone in the darkness of evening in order to catch up to their unit advancing deeper into battle.

Field medics found him a day later and took him to the field hospital from where he was transferred to a regular hospital about 100 miles behind the lines. His wounds healed, and now he has a Purple Heart.

Ernest was the first man from Otter Tail County to be wounded in the war, and as such was a hero. When he came home on furlough with his new bride, I was very proud of him. I also liked his wife. By then I was fourteen and had finally outgrown my desire to be a pest.

Our neighborhood and our county sent many young men to the Armed Services. Many had been honored in the local Sons of Norway hall by a farewell dance. It's amazing the floor there held out through years of polkas and schottisches. I can still visualize that bobbing floor! Some returned to dance there again, and others did not. Sorrow touched everyone in some manner during those years. I lost a cousin and several acquaintances, but my hero, Cpl. Ernest Hanson, came home.

The War Years

Eddie Albert was the lead character in the first movie I saw when I was twelve. I remember the second movie better. It starred Stan Laurel and Oliver Hardy. Laurel was tall, slim, and somewhat child-like while Hardy was short, plump and prone to getting into trouble. I laughed until my sides ached. The cartoons following the main feature were super, too. I had not seen cartoons before, and every move they made seemed to tickle me. Everyone laughed heartily over moves that would not evoke a chuckle now. We are so used to that kind of comedy that we no longer appreciate it.

Our family prospered as World War II progressed. Even so, I could not afford to go to a movie every Saturday night, and I had to make hard choices from the list of coming attractions. I was encouraged by my parents to see such movies as *My Friend Flicka*, *Lassie Come Home*, and *Bambi*. But I also saw the wonderful *How Green Was My Valley* and the great war movie, *Mrs. Miniver.* The latter was a story of an English housewife who encountered a downed German pilot in her back yard during a blitz over London.

The saddest movie I ever saw was *The Sullivan Brothers* about five brothers in one Iowa family who lost their lives when their ship was torpedoed and sunk. Not a man or woman emerged from the theatre that night with dry eyes. After this tragedy, the Armed Forces forbade siblings being together in combat units.

One thing I did afford on a weekly basis was an ice cream cone. We could buy three dips for a nickel. I had a hard time choosing three of the several delectable flavors: strawberry, chocolate, orange, lime, grape and vanilla.

The little theatre in Battle Lake had to install blackout curtains at considerable expense. They had to be drawn over the huge windows whenever the lights were to be used if a general blackout had been ordered. I wonder now whether the greater purpose may have been to make the populace feel patriotic and helpful in the war effort. A tiny town like Battle Lake couldn't do much to guide incoming enemy aircraft!

Sometimes there were war bond movies which could be seen only by purchasing a war bond as the admission price. The least expensive bond cost $18.75 and had a maturity value of $25.00.

Well into the war there began to be War Bond Rallies held in many communities. I went to one such rally in Battle Lake at which the featured speaker was young, handsome Captain Einar Mikkelson of the Flying Tigers under General Chennault. Officially, that group was not a part of our Armed Services war effort. They were a group of American volunteer pilots who came to the aid of China in its war against Japan prior to the attack on Pearl Harbor. Captain Mikkelson spent a year and a half in China and India. He fought out of Rangoon, Burma, bombing and strafing the Japanese who were advancing up the Burma Road toward Kunming. Eventually he saw Rangoon fall to the enemy. The Flying Tigers were disbanded when the U.S. Army took over. Captain Mikkelson joined the war effort under the Chinese national government where he felt he could be of greater service, and he lost his life flying over the Himalayas. Fergus Falls honored their famous son by naming their airport Einar Mikkelson Field. For many years now I am saddened to drive by and see that it currently bears the name, Fergus Falls Municipal Airport. How dull! And how soon we forget!

We were encouraged over the radio and through the newspapers and agricultural magazines as well as by the County Home Extension publications to plant Victory Gardens. It would teach us to feed ourselves in case of war and hardship on our soil, and it would ease possible food shortages.

We collected scrap metals for the war effort, even aluminum foil and the aluminum tips of shoe laces. Children were encouraged to collect the fluff in milkweed pods to stuff life jackets.

Flour came in pretty cotton print sacks for some years. Homemakers were told to use the sacks to sew quilts and clothing, sheets and pillowcases.

Sugar was rationed, and we all signed up for ration booklets. Most of our sugar came from Hawaii, and there was a real fear that we would not get any from there if the bombing there were repeated. Gasoline, rubber tires, rubber boots, shoes, and coffee were also rationed. I still save my unused ration book.

Nylon hosiery was brought home by servicemen. One of my high school teachers got two pair from her husband, and they were an immediate hit, despite the dark seam down the back. Until then, ladies' hosiery was made of rayon. My sister got married in 1948 and sewed some of her wedding finery from a white nylon parachute her fiance brought home.

The jet plane resulted when aviation necessity became the mother of invention. The first plane using a practical turbojet was flown in Great Britain in 1941. Bell Aircraft Corporation in the United States built a plane that used two turbojets and tested it in 1942. That year the Germans flew the first successful jet combat plane. We wanted to catch up. At last, in 1947 the United States had the first jet plane to fly faster than sound travels. It was launched from an airborne bomber and was piloted by Charles Yeager. I was thrilled to hear about it.

The war was the era of the big bands like Glen Miller, Wayne King, and Sammy Kaye. Irving Berlin gave us "White Christmas" which Bing Crosby sang so beautifully for us, and Kate Smith belted out Berlin's "God Bless America."

The economy improved during the war, and the Depression was forgotten. Prices for goods climbed, and there were new jobs and no real unemployment. My parents sold their big turkey flock in 1945 and paid off the farm mortgage at last.

When Franklin D. Roosevelt died, the whole nation mourned. We got the news on the radio. Then someone called asking me to report to the high school for a memorial service because I was in the high school choir. FDR had aged terribly, like Lincoln did during the Civil War, and we all felt sad that he could not have lived to see Japan surrender on September 2, 1945.

All through those war years I wrote letters to servicemen and got the tiny 4"x5" V-Mail air-letters back from those stationed overseas. They were always censored with telling words or lines deleted, and they were photographed to this small size to save room in transit.

I did a lot of praying for relatives and neighbors and anyone I knew in the military service. I walked the quarter mile to our mailbox during summer school vacations and prayed as I walked that the headlines in the *Fergus Falls Daily Journal* would bear good news. Often it was bad, such as the Battle of the Bulge in which I lost a cousin. The personal tragic stories of men and women wounded, missing in action or killed appeared throughout the paper. I often shed tears as I walked homeward, reading. I remember feeling tense and worried.

Each of us experienced the war years on a very personal level, each in a different way. Some, like me, were lucky to have had no parent or sibling in the war, and for some their only major sacrifice was one of worry and frazzled nerves. We owe so very much to those who made the real sacrifices!

Mindy's War Ration Book

V-Mail Letters, World War II

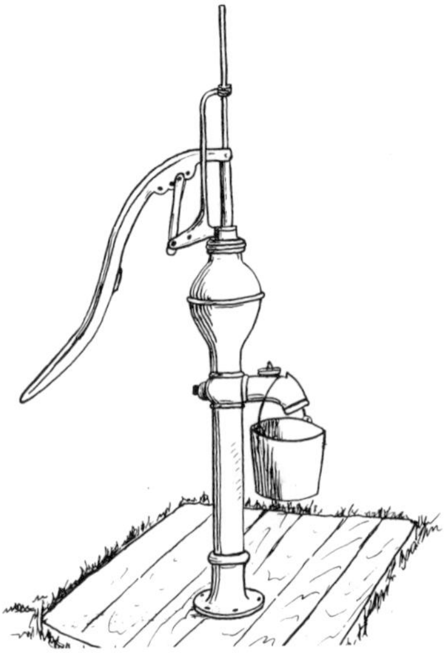

The School Pump

Mindy Teaches School

My high school graduation in '47 was followed by a summer of moving off the farm. My parents had an auction sale, and almost all our antiques were sold because Mother had no appreciation for "that old junk." Her generation was looking for something they had never had, something modern with simple, straight lines. Severely modern, blond furniture was popular at this time, for it was a break away from the dark, walnut finishes everyone had grown up with.

Early that spring I had settled on teachers' training for my next phase of education. My mother had missed one chance at a teaching career, and that was her lifelong disappointment. She had only an eighth grade education, but when she was a young lady, she had been asked to teach in a rural school in eastern North Dakota. She would have had to live alone and board herself in the school building. Her adamant parents would not hear of having their young daughter live alone on the prairie since the neighbors were a mile or more away from the school. Mother always felt that she had lost out on a career because of this, so she hoped that I would become a teacher.

I did not feel pressured into teaching. It seemed at that time that girls became teachers, nurses or beauticians. A few, like my sister, had become a medical secretary and technician. No one I had ever known had become a lady pilot, a lady physician, or a lady lawyer. There seemed to be few choices.

I started the teachers' training course of nine months in Fergus Falls before my parents were ready to move into their home in that city, and I stayed with Aunt Mabel and Uncle Lorence. We had a good time together that month, and then I moved in with my parents who moved to a house on South Mill Street where they were to be city dwellers for the first time.

In the spring the class was ready for practice teaching. I was assigned to rural school district 285 north of Ashby, Minnesota. I enjoyed my two weeks there so much that I was overjoyed when the school board accepted me for the position of teacher for the following term.

I got room and board in the homes of my pupils, first with one family, the Joruds, then with another family, the Smedsruds. My landlady, Mrs. Jorud, came down with mumps and was quite ill after that first Christmas vacation, and the school board did not want the teacher exposed to her in fear that she would get the mumps and that school would have to close for two weeks. So I had to go to live with the Bakke family for those two weeks while Mrs. Jorud recovered.

Two wonderful years were spent in that school and community among friendly people and charming children. I taught all eight grades, but only six classes had anyone enrolled each year. I walked two full miles to school each day in good weather and bad, arriving at the little square building about 7:30 a.m., and I went right to stoking up the fire that I managed to keep going constantly in the furnace. I took the axe and split my own kindling wood, shoveled the coal needed, and shoveled out the ashes into a pail and disposed of that in the outdoor toilet.

School District 285

While I was not the janitor as far as cleaning the building was concerned, I frequently washed the hall floor after muddy boots had turned it into a gritty mess. Self-reliance was necessary.

I did not own a car. To get home to my parents I had to find a ride by car to Battle Lake to get on the bus to Fergus Falls. My father brought me back on Sunday evening.

Just as we had P.T.A. meetings and Field Day, spelling contests and music festivals, school picnics and Parents' Visiting Day in the rural school I had attended, I was now in charge of these same activities. The older pupils prepared exhibits for the Otter Tail County Fair, and I enjoyed helping them with these projects.

The Minnesota Territorial Centennial was celebrated in 1949 with a big community program. I remember wearing my Grandmother Berit's black blouse with black beadwork on it and my mother's long black wool skirt. My hair was wound up in a pug at the back, and my feet suffered in narrow, pointed-toe, high top, laced shoes. I truly looked the part of the 1849 school marm!

The highlight of the term was the school Christmas program. I gave it my all. Father came and helped me put up the smooth wires on which to hang the burlap stage curtains I had labored long and hard to sew. A school board member came and put up the stage. This was done right after Thanksgiving vacation in order to allow for practice of the 4 or 5 plays we had decided upon. Regular daily work had to be completed first, and sometimes we got in extra practice during the noon hour. Children were assigned recitations, musical solos, and character parts in plays about six weeks before Christmas. During the last week before the program we devoted two hours at the end of each day's classes to going through the entire program.

There were costumes to be designed and to request the parents to make, stage props to locate, and innumerable details to attend to.

Two weeks before the program the names of every adult in the community were put into a pail, and the older children drew names for a gift exchange for the entire school district. These they delivered after school. Every adult took part. The school children had a separate drawing in which any preschool child who wished to could also take part. Very small children were furnished a small gift by the parent so that they would not be left out. A token gift for about 50 cents was the expectation.

At last the long-awaited evening arrived. Teacher and pupils

Mindy as a Teacher, Age 22

alike had flushed cheeks and beaming faces. All were dressed in their best clothing. The program would be nearly two hours in duration. Seldom did any child miss a cue or a line or in any way goof an assigned part. It was great to see and hear the talent those children possessed.

When the applause died down after the last curtain call, Santa came into the room, dressed in his splendid red suit, calling "Ho! Ho! Ho!" His big belly shook as he laughed, and it had to be given an occasional upward boost. He had two or three helpers, and all the community gifts were given out from under the tree. Santa called out each by name and recognized each and every one. My school board gave me an alarm clock! No, I had never been late for anything. Each child was given a bag of peanuts and candy from the school district, and every child in attendance was given a shiny red apple.

The walls of that square schoolroom seemed to bulge from the strain of so many bodies, so much activity, and the din of loud conversation and laughter. Coffee, Kool Aid, and cake were served, and little by little small tired children dropped off to sleep in a chair or on a parent's lap, signaling that it was time to find the family car and head homeward.

Recess time was perhaps the favorite time of the day for most pupils, and it was my favorite, too, at certain times of the year. I loved to teach the old games and relays that I had known as a child. Games such as *Last Couple Out* and *Tin Can Off* or *Captain, May I* were favorites.

Modern day children are taught ball games and gymnastics, but the emphasis is on winning, not on having fun with other children and learning to get along with them. The modern child plays against his or her own age group, but the rural school child learned to socialize with all ages and to respect children of every age level and to have fun with them. Many important skills can be learned through these fun games.

Although I later taught in city schools, my two years spent teaching this rural school is one of the richest experiences of my life, and I wish that this way of life had continued for rural children. It was a good way to educate, and I knew many skillful, warm teachers who inspired their pupils and brought out the best in them.

My First Real Trip

My rural school was dismissed for the 1949 term, and I assumed vacation would be totally boring. I had to go home to live with my parents for the summer because I could not afford to live anywhere else. I was saving my money for college.

The *Fergus Falls Daily Journal* lay on a small table in our living room, and I picked it up to skim its pages. An ad jumped out from a page. It said, "Wanted: riders to Seattle to share gas. Leaving June 30th. Call 736-6506." I brought the paper into the kitchen to my mother because I knew she had long desired to go to Seattle to visit her only sister, a working spinster. Mother seemed interested but pessimistic.

After considerable nagging on my part, she called the number in the ad. A major trucking company semi driver who was on his vacation, a single man, wanted to drive to Seattle and wanted to take riders to share gasoline costs, as the ad stated. He sounded friendly and humorous, and an experienced truck driver ought to be a good driver, Mother reasoned. My usually cautious mother discussed it with my father for less than an hour before deciding that I could ride out with him, because an elderly man and a local sixteen-year old girl were also riding with him. Mother felt she could not get ready to go so quickly as it was already June 28th. Only a day and a half to prepare! She would take the train out four days later, and we would meet at Aunt Ida's home in Seattle.

Ray soon impressed me as a good driver, and he was a very funny man. It was pure entertainment to be in his company. I liked Sylvia, the teen-age girl, too. She and I rode in the back seat of his '47 Chevrolet.

We drove to Fargo and headed west on highway 10. It was very narrow by today's standards with grassy edges where the interstate highways have blacktop shoulders. I remember flinching whenever we met a big truck. The wheels of a semi would fill the whole lane, and as we passed one another, the suction tended to pull us toward the center of the road.

We were coming into Valley City, North Dakota, when the two men commented on what a pretty place this was. That June the hills around the city were brown and gray. Not a blade of truly green grass could be seen. I thought it to be the most God-forsaken place I had ever laid eyes on. I wouldn't know what forsaken really meant until we would get into hot, dusty, eastern Montana where I doubted a rattlesnake could survive.

Just west of Valley City we passed a prairie lake in which two adult men were bathing very close to the road. Their old truck was parked at the road edge. As we drove past, Ray honked, and the men stood up and splashed water on each other. They were totally naked! They were the first naked men I had ever seen, and the men in our car were embarrassed and apologetic.

There was no air conditioning in the cars at that time, but the open windows brought in plenty of fresh air–and grasshoppers. One got into the back of my mouth and got stuck so that I had to cough and gag to get it out. The temperature in eastern Montana that day was 98 degrees, so we decided to take a hotel for the night in Glendive.

We should have stayed on highway 10 and driven to Deer Lodge for the second night, but for some forgotten reason, we got onto Alternate 10 and got hotel rooms in Philipsburg, Montana. Sylvia and I had a room on the second floor, street side. As I entered, the door knob came off in my hand, so Ray went to the lady at the desk for some tools and repaired the knob and the lock before we girls could retire. I had a hard time getting to sleep due to a blinking red neon sign outside our windows.

In the middle of the night and in the middle of our most sound sleep, Sylvia and I were awakened by the sound of galloping hooves, whooping, and yelling. We ran to the window to see a trio of horsemen and nags making their way along the lighted main street. The riders had no doubt been enlivened by too much socializing behind those swinging louvered doors.

The next day brought us into the Rocky Mountains. I had never seen mountains before, so I did not waste time napping. I stayed awake, staring out the window, not wanting to miss a tall peak or a sharp curve in the winding road. I thought Mullen, Idaho, was a real wild-west town, sandwiched between two high ridges. Even today, there is barely room for an elevated interstate highway through there.

We deviated northward to see Steamboat Rock, and when Sylvia read the sign for Soap Lake as "Soup Lake," I thought Ray would choke on his spittle! We seemed to slide down the steep switchbacks into Grand Coulee Dam. The power houses looked like small shoeboxes below the 550-foot spillways, and inside one power house, nine huge turbines dwarfed us.

We drove into the night to reach the Cascades west of

Wenatche, Washington. There we pulled the car onto a road turn-off and slept. It got quite chilly, so the cold awakened us early.

Coming into Seattle, I was really out of my element. The city looked white as most of the houses were white or light in color, and it seemed cluttered with houses too close together and bare for want of trees. I made note of the seven hills, like the seven hills of Rome.

Ray brought the two other passengers to their destinations, and then he found my aunt's apartment somewhere in the neighborhood of the Seattle Art Museum. I paid him my share of gasoline for the trip: $10.00. The total cost was about $40 for the entire trip out.

My aunt took me to Woodland Park to see the rose gardens and zoo, to the Seattle Art Museum, and to the waterfront where we ate in Iver Haaglund's Acres of Clams. I discovered I had an instant attraction for piers and boats, seafood restaurants and squawking seagulls.

Ray and I met my mother at the train depot when her train rolled in, and a day or two later Ray came to get Mother, Aunt Ida, and me. We had a wonderful, all-day trip to Mount Rainier and Paradise Inn. The very narrow, curving road up the mountain nearly caused my heart to stand still. Once up there it was such fun to try walking on the slippery, melting snowfields! The aroma of the evergreens and the brightness of the snow-and glacier-covered peak are unforgettable. Avalanche lilies were in bloom among the melting snowdrifts.

On the way down we visited Snoqualmie Falls which had a very heavy volume of white water gushing over the top.

When the time came to go home a few days later, Ray wanted to take a more southerly route. We crossed the scenic Columbia River Gorge, visited the fish ladder at Bonneville Dam, and headed for Salt Lake City. It was an impressive, rich-looking city from the Utah state capitol steps, and we took in the Mormon Temple grounds and an organ concert there before heading for Cheyenne and the Black Hills.

The varied country kept me spellbound. The dryness, the heat, the absence of green color, the sharply-curving, narrow roads, often without guard rails, stand out in my memory. We also saw some working cowboys near Cheyenne.

Driving through part of the Black Hills at night, tearing up a steep hill, Ray had to stop abruptly to avoid hitting a bull bison lying across the center line. Only after the bull discovered that our head lights were not going to go away did he pull his bulk up and mosey into the ditch.

The faces of Mt. Rushmore were great, and the pigtail bridges were a very special experience, as was the Needle's Eye. We stayed in the old Alex Johnson Hotel in Rapid City that night. It was very hot in the hotel so that keeping the window open all night helped only a little.

Aunt Ida, Mother May, and Mindy at Snoqualmie Falls Near Seattle

We dipped south to drive through the South Dakota Badlands where Ray worried about whether or not he would need water for the radiator in that heat, but he made it to Wall Drug, then only a fraction of what it is today, and checked the radiator. If it had been hot in the hotel, it was starting to get much hotter. It reached 102 degrees as we crossed South Dakota that afternoon, and the hot wind was so searing that we shut the car windows to make it more tolerable. Only the Burma Shave signs along the road relieved the monotony of the trip across South Dakota: "I use it too, the bald man said–It makes my face just like my head." "Train wrecks few–Reason clear–Fireman never hugs engineer." "Hat and tie, nice and clean–Space between spoiled the scene."

It was a brutal ending to an otherwise great eighteen day trip.

Just before getting home to Fergus Falls, Ray told us he'd had an accident with his truck in Minneapolis, and that he was off-duty while the accident was being investigated. It was not a vacation.

"It was a brand-new semi on it's first trip out," he said. "I took a shortcut through the Twin Cities by going an unfamiliar route that crossed an unmarked railroad track behind a huge warehouse. A speeding train hit the semi so fast that the trailer tipped away from the cab and it was demolished. Luckily, I wasn't hurt." He chuckled as he told the story.

"I was hauling eggs... a full load of eggs," he laughed, "and you should have seen the train locomotive! Egg yolks were dripping all over down the front of the locomotive."

Ray could still see the humor in a situation that could have cost him his job, if not his life. In time he was cleared of responsibility for the accident and was reinstated on the job. Seeing what a skillful driver he was, I am sure it was a correct decision.

Thanks to Ray, Mother got to visit her sister in Seattle, and Mother and I had this one wonderful trip together. The trip holds a special place in my memory, and it launched me on a lifetime of travel.

Ships and Seas

The *M. S. Oslofjord* was the newest passenger ship in the Norwegian-America Line fleet in 1953 when I first sailed on her to Norway.

"Rolling seas" took on new meaning for me on the third day out from New York. I was seated for dinner in the ship's dining room when the first huge swell hit the ship broadside. As I looked out the big squarish windows to starboard, I saw the sea disappear, leaving only sky. A glance across the room to portside showed the sea's horizon rising up the windows to disappear above them. The ship hesitated a second or two and then reversed itself. In that lunge of the ship, a lady's chair tipped over, depositing her on the floor. I turned to look at her, as did everyone else, and seven other chairs and people overturned.

I heard shrieks of both fear and laughter as the waiters went into frenzied action, fastening all the chairs to the floor by hooking a chain under each one to floor hooks. Having secured the chairs, they propped up narrow boards along the edges of the tables and grabbed water pitchers and wet down the linen tablecloths to keep the flatware and dishes on the tables.

Meanwhile, the *M.S.Oslofjord* kept rolling from side to side. We were informed by the dining room steward that the ship had encountered huge swells set off by a hurricane in the Caribbean which explained this tempest on a sunny day with bright blue sky overhead.

An opened wine bottle standing in a niche in the wall fell on its side, sending forth a stream of red wine to the floor. I watched as the wine continued across the room, then returned with another listing of the ship. Flatware slid across dinner plates to the floor, and stemmed goblets overturned and rolled around.

It was a bit difficult to eat as the fork didn't always accurately find my mouth on the first attempt. Besides that, I was busy laughing at the waiters walking with one short leg and one leg outstretched as they leaned against the listing of the ship while balancing a huge tray of food on one hand and shoulder, stepping over rolling bottles and ladies' handbags on the floor.

I saw nothing but hilarity in this sudden bedlam, but several fearful passengers got up and left for their staterooms as if they would find firm ground there.

My traveling companion, Donna, and I left the dining room after the meal to go to the dance floor in midships. We discovered the difficulty of walking on a rolling floor. As we approached two easy chairs at the edge of the dance floor, one of them took off, sliding with increasing momentum across the room. It was followed closely by the round cage on a stand used to hold Bingo letters.

All this was very funny to me, but dancing proved to be even more hilarious. Doing a swinging polka was downright dangerous, so the ship's orchestra wisely switched to playing slow waltzes and two-steps.

Disembarkation was in Oslo where we were met by my mother's cousin, Halvor Smestad, and his nephew, Leif Smestad. We spent two weeks visiting them and other relatives, and we traveled throughout Valdres and the fjord country to Bergen.

We found ourselves on another ship crossing the North Sea from Bergen to England. This time it stormed. The ship pitched and groaned. The forward end shot up out of the water while the aft rode low. Then it reversed itself. This violent elevator motion made walking up the gangway stairs great fun. The steps seemed either to run down and away from my feet, or my feet came down hard on each step as if weighted by lead.

Most of the passengers and a third of the crew had to "feed the fish." I was surprised that I came through the storm without a hint of seasickness.

After exploring the British Isles, we traveled in ten countries on the continent, terminating our visit in Paris. As our tour bus rolled down the Champs Elysées that first evening, the main architectural wonders of the city were flood-lit and impressive. Paris was truly beautiful that night!

The next morning a national strike went into effect. Public buildings and monuments were no longer flood-lit in the evenings. Bakers did not bake, garbage collectors did not collect, postmen did not deliver. Using any mail services or sending a telegram or telephoning was impossible. Banks were closed. Busses, trains and planes stood still. The only transportation available was the taxicabs as they were privately owned.

Our tour was to leave France in five days. We stayed in Hotel Reynold near the Arc d' Triomphe, so we enjoyed Paris on foot as best we could, leaving our problems to the tour guide. While we visited the Louvre Art Museum and the Cathedral of

Notre Dame, the tour guide hired a private taxi driver to take him into Belgium where he contracted for a big bus to come to Paris to rescue us.

We realized how fortunate we were to be with a large tour group as we drove out of central Paris past numerous tourists sleeping on their luggage in the streets. They were stranded, unable to leave the city, and too broke to pay for a hotel room. Among the tourists draped over their luggage were piles of reeking garbage.

Our tour guide had sent a telegram from Belgium to the *RMS Queen Elizabeth I*. That world's largest ocean liner waited in the outer Cherbourg harbor six hours for our group to arrive! That ship was too large to dock at the Cherbourg piers, so we rode tenders out to the ship to get on board. I was overwhelmed by her huge size, looking like a floating city as she lay well-lighted in the otherwise dark outer harbor. I was also lost much of the way home among nearly 800 tourist class passengers; I was not permitted in first class. She could carry some over 2,000 passengers and 1,280 officers and crew members, * but she never had a full load.

The *RMS Queen Elizabeth I* is still the world's largest ocean liner ever built, just a very few feet longer than her sister ship, the *Queen Mary*. Tragically, both the lovely *M.S. Oslofjord* and the grand *RMS Queen Elizabeth I* burned and are resting at the bottom of the sea.

*From *The Elizabeth: Passage of a Queen* by Leonard A. Stevens

Pioneering the Alcan

The Moorhead State College geography department offered a tour to Alaska for credit in July, 1958, and I was traveling as a student participant. Professor Harold Addicott traveled with us and gave us some informal instruction enroute. We were to travel up the Alaska Highway, then known as the Alcan Highway, to Alaska to explore the state and to reside in a dormitory on the University of Alaska campus near Fairbanks for one week. Here we would attend day-long classes in Alaskan geology, geography, flora and fauna.

All this depended upon our getting through to Fairbanks,

and if we succeeded, Professor Addicott said, we would make history as the first Greyhound bus ever to make its way up the Alcan all the way to Fairbanks.

To ensure our success, Jim Drury of Moorhead, a Greyhound charter driver, had been hired to drive the bus. He had recently completed one week of special training at Greyhound's Minneapolis shop in the mechanics of this particular bus. Jim had selected the older style bus with the small windows that was in use before the Scenicruisers. This was because it had sturdy springs under it instead of the air bellows used on the newer buses. It would stand up better on rough gravel roads.

Extra tires and certain spare parts were carried with the bus in anticipation of a breakdown. We would be lucky if we had no breakdowns and if no heavy rains came to cause swollen creeks to wash out the highway. It would take many days to bring in heavy equipment and repair such damage.

We left Minnesota on July 27th, traveling via Great Falls, Calgary, and Edmonton. At Edmonton we drove to the Greyhound bus garage for a maintenance reason. It was quite full of buses, and Jim had to wait at the entrance while a Canadian driver was trying unsuccessfully to turn his bus and maneuver it into a tight place.

Jim opened the little side window and asked him, "You mind if I have a go at it?"

"Be my guest!" said the unhappy driver.

Jim was behind the wheel in seconds and expertly put that bus into place in a bus garage he was totally unfamiliar with. We knew then why he had been selected as our driver.

About 50 miles out of Edmonton we found ourselves on a long stretch of road construction that was really difficult for Jim to drive over and punishing to the bus and tires. Stones varying from the size of chicken eggs to baseballs covered the road bed, and finer gravel had not yet been applied. I had never seen this kind of construction anywhere, and there must have been 40 miles of it.

Suddenly a stone struck our windshield as a truck passed us. It came right into our bus, barely missing the driver's face and spraying tiny bits of glass all over those of us sitting in the two front seats. It left a half-dollar size hole and a huge spider web pattern on the windshield. And we hadn't even come to the start of the Alcan yet!

We stopped at a Grande Prairie gas station to sweep up the broken glass. We would just have to put up with the cracks and the hole in the windshield.

Dawson Creek, British Columbia, was a dusty little city with gravel streets and no curbs and gutters when I arrived there on August 1, 1958. Many homes and public buildings were unpainted and weatherbeaten. I saw scarcely a grassy lawn anywhere. The whole place reminded me of the Wild West towns in the movies.

A tour of the city revealed a few new and modern buildings, too. Down town boasted a new Hudson's Bay Company department store. There were some attractive churches and fine schools.

Because some of my fellow travelers and I were teachers, we visited the Dawson Creek Elementary School and were impressed with the new equipment such as large greenboards which I had not yet seen in Minnesota schools. Something else was new to us: in all the rooms hung a portrait of Queen Elizabeth, of course. No Abraham Lincoln or George Washington here!

In the center of Dawson Creek and in the middle of the street stood Milepost 0. This white wooden post marked the very beginning of the 1, 523-mile Alcan Highway. 1,221 miles of this highway crosses Canada. Construction on the Alcan was started during World War II as the only military supply route to Alaska by land from the 48 states, but the war ended before its completion.

Minnesotans appreciate evergreen trees, but we grew weary of seeing only trees, trees, and more trees all the way to Fort Nelson on our first day on the Alcan. Little did we know that the forest borders the Alcan nearly all the way.

The placid Peace River flowed through our route. When we approached the big Peace River bridge, we saw that a segment involving about a third of the bridge had fallen into the river like a crumpled ribbon so that the bridge spanned only two-thirds of the river! We had heard that a bad storm had passed through here. Had we come so far to be turned back because a storm had knocked out the bridge? Our hearts sank! The Alcan was the only way through here.

Jim, however, was not about to give up so easily. He looked around at the river, the forest, and the railroad trestle some hundred yards down the road. The trestle spanned the Peace River. He took the bus to the railroad bridge and got out to look. One could tell by the clipped grass blades at the start of the bridge that it had been used recently. It looked totally sound, and yes, it was wide enough, just barely. Could it carry the weight of the bus? Why not, it carried trains loaded with heavy road equipment.

He could maneuver the big curve in the trestle, but would there be a train coming through here today? It was totally quiet out here, making it easy to hear a train in the distance. Freight trains would not travel over 30 mph through here with a curving trestle coming up.

Jim sent Roger, a young man, to the far end of the bridge–perhaps 1000 feet–to get down and put his ear to the steel track to listen for the rumbling of an approaching train. Then Jim drove the bus very slowly and carefully on the railroad tracks across that trestle. I think everyone on the bus prayed, but I also looked out my window to see the dark water far below.

When he stopped at the far end to pick up Roger, the passengers cheered wildly.

We pulled up at our Fort Nelson Hotel in late afternoon. Everyone wanted to know how we had gotten through, but Jim was not telling. He borrowed an air compressor and blew the inch of dust from the rear end of the bus, then from our suitcases in the compartment under the bus.

Pioneering Greyhound Bus to Alaska, 1958, and Pearl Lunde, Mindy's Roommate

Fort Nelson was not an incorporated village but just a settlement that got its start as a Hudson's Bay Company trading post. Indians, road crews, gas station attendents, hotel operators and some transitory people lived there.

Our hotel offered fair food, tolerable beds, lots of noise, and a half-dozen bath tubs with very rust-colored running water. We took turns getting the rooms with bath, and this night I had a bath tub to share with four roommates. As Jim handed us our room keys, he said he'd drop by after 7:00 for his bath. Everyone laughed.

At about 7:30 p.m., Jim knocked hard on our door and shouted, "I'm here for my bath now!"

An older lady in our group was in the tub, and did she get out of that tub in a hurry! Water flew everywhere as she scrambled for a towel. Jim, of course, was long gone down the hall, chuckling, no doubt. His humor added fun to our trip.

The next morning was Sunday, so we attended worship services in the simple wooden Anglican Church which was built up on four feet like a trapper's cache to avoid being chewed into by rodents. It was kept open only during summer and was serviced by a student priest.

We drove over Summit Pass, the highest point on the Alcan at 4,250 feet.

We inspected a real trapper's cache beside Muncho Lake. The lake is long and narrow, backed by high forest-covered mountains. Here we saw a pickup with a camper pulling out and driving ahead of us. On the back of the camper was a home-made sign that read, "Have wife, must travel." We argued over the precise meaning of that sign for the next two days as that pickup was seen ahead of us from time to time.

We got off the bus and walked across the bridge over the Liard River, the only suspension bridge on the Alcan. It was nearly a quarter-mile long, and the view of the reflective Liard River made the walk worthwhile. It felt good, too, to shake a leg.

Engineers and construction crews building the Alcan from the west had come together with crews building the road from the Dawson Creek end at a place named Contact Creek. Here they met on September 23, 1948. It is 588.1 miles from Dawson Creek. We paused there for pictures and to reflect on the 300 miles we had come so far that day. The highway was all gravel, and the going was sometimes slow and wash-board rough, always very dusty. We had spotted only one deer and one black bear along the seemingly endless forest. There were no signs of human habitation for 60 mile stretches and no settlements between the places where we stayed the night.

As we rode, we sang, read books or slept to fill the hours.

We spent the night at Lower Post, an old Indian village. In addition to services personnel and Indians it had some professional people because it had a new mission boarding school for 290 girls. The village was a series of wooden buildings strung out along either side of the highway for two or three blocks.

The next morning Jim nailed our sign to Signposts beyond Lower Post. Crewmen building the Alcan were the first to post a sign there from their home town. It became a tradition for travelers. There must have been close to eighty signs there on several tall posts. Our sign read, "Moorhead State College, Moorhead, Minnesota," and an arrow pointed to the southeast.

Beyond was a huge forest fire west from Watson Lake all the way to Swift River, a distance of about 100 miles. It no doubt burned much more territory than we could see, but for that entire distance we drove through charred forest and burning, crackling trees on both sides of the highway.

A tree would smoulder for a time as the sap-filled trunk burned, and then the whole green top would ignite in a red blaze, making a firecracker sound as it ignited. Smoke was very thick in some areas. I questioned the sanity of continuing to press forward in this ever-increasing inferno. The gravel highway was wide, but I feared having a burning tree fall on us. It was also terribly depressing to see all that destruction!

In British Columbia there were about 390 known fires so far that summer, and in the Yukon Territory about 200,000 square miles had burned at that time in 1958. Animals would catch on fire, run, drop dead, and start a new fire where they fell. There was no attempt seen at putting out these fires. They burned out naturally as there were no other roads, no airstrips, no equipment, and no crews to fight the fires. Lightning was said to cause many of them.

At last we came to Teslin Lake and Nisutlin Bay Bridge, the largest bridge on the Alcan. The lake is 80 miles long and is named for the Teslin Indians. Lakes and rivers were the major breaks in the monotony of the thick forest.

I have forgotten the location, but somewhere not far from there we had a light lunch at a tiny roadside cafe beside a creek. The Alcan dipped down rather sharply there, crossed the creek on an unbelievably tiny bridge, and rose sharply on the other side. It had rained during the night, so the proprieter of the cafe said to Jim, "You're not going to cross that flimsy bridge with that big busload of people!"

Jim removed his Greyhound cap and scratched his bald head. He didn't say anything–very unusual for Jim. He then walked across the bridge, which was not a whole lot longer than the bus, to inspect the other end. A few people were already back on the bus when he came back, and he ordered them to get off. Then Jim seated himself behind the steering wheel and kept the passenger door open as he drove the empty bus across the bridge. The bridge only creaked a little. Jim waved to us to come over and board while the cafe proprieter now scratched his head in amazement. We all entered the bus singing "For He's a Jolly Good Fellow."

We descended a long, steep hill into Whitehorse that day, a real shack town, I thought, although there was a new government building and a new school. We stayed two nights there, giving us a free day to rest from long days of constant riding. We also explored the town, visiting the retired old Yukon River stern-wheelers and going to see the MacBride Museum in a log house. To my surprise the museum was excellent. I especially enjoyed seeing the primitive wood and stone carvings made by Indians.

On August 6 we drove through more burned forest before coming to Kluane Lake, the largest in the Yukon Territory, about 50 miles long. It was full of lake trout and Arctic greyling, we were told. I was more interested in the placid water mirroring the pastel blues and greys of the surrounding treeless mountains. They looked smooth and bald. It was an unforgettably beautiful scene that made the long ride here worthwhile.

Later we passed by the St. Elias Range before crossing the Alaska border and arriving at Forty Mile Roadhouse. Here regular gas that was $.28 a gallon back home was $.89. We had driven 385 miles that day, and we needed to fill the tank. While Jim did that, we got acquainted with thirty-some huskies chained beside their dog houses.

The next three days were spent traveling to explore Valdez and the Columbia Glacier before heading north. We arrived in Fairbanks, and we had at last conquered the Alcan Highway by Greyhound bus and reached our destination! We celebrated that event by eating out as a group.

A 47-passenger Wien Alaska plane took our group to Fort Yukon the next day. It was the largest Indian village in Alaska with about 300 Athabascan families. It lay on the grey, treeless Yukon River bank, eight miles above the Arctic Circle.

Before crossing the Arctic Circle, the stewardess carefully checked our seatbelts and then strapped herself to a seat. The pilot suddenly put the plane into a nose dive, and as soon as I realized what he was doing, he pulled us back up. My head first hit the head rest hard, and my facial skin was pulled back toward my ears. A lady's purse floated weightless above my head before landing on my lap. I don't need to tell you where my stomach was! This, the pilot said on the intercom, was to initiate us into the Club of Arctic Explorers.

Fort Yukon had a log post office with moose antlers mounted above the apex of the roof. The town's water boy, a grown Indian man, was seen pulling a cart of huge bottles of fresh water, delivering them to the residents.

Fort Yukon had one modern, non-log building, the public school. It was wonderfully furnished and equipped and would have been a teacher's paradise in Minnesota. The superintendent, originally from Ohio, offered me a teaching position there. The salary was great, and I was tempted as I liked the Athabascan children I had met. My food for the entire winter would have to be shipped up on a container barge from Seattle in the fall. I dared not plan meals for nine months that closely, and I hated powdered milk, so I declined the offer.

The week of classes at the University was most interesting. We panned for gold in the Chatanika River, watched placer mining, and studied the permafrost. We picked wild blueberries in the wilderness and attended the Tanana County Fair. Jim drove us to these places and stayed in the dormitory with our group. Many of us had a clear but distant view of Mt. McKinley from our rooms.

Those evenings in the dorm were relaxing and fun. Most of our group were students in their thirties or older as they were the ones who could more easily afford such a trip. Five of us were younger, and we livened up dormitory life by short-sheeting one another's beds and putting a small rock in someone's pillowcase. Jim went to bed to discover something fragrant making him sneeze over and over. He turned on the light to find Blue Cheer detergent sprinkled over his pillow inside the pillow case! He got his revenge in clever ways.

We had to say goodbye to Jim when we took the train to Palmer to study farming in the Matanuska Valley. We later explored Anchorage and flew to Juneau.

Congress approved statehood for Alaska on June 30, 1958, but Alaska entered the union on January 3, 1959. While in Juneau the incoming territorial governor of Alaska held a reception for the outgoing governor at the Governor's Mansion. He invited our group to the reception. We walked from the Baranof Hotel in the pouring rain and rang the doorbell. The host governor greeted the soaked, bedraggled-looking group from Minnesota. Soon we were mingling with champagne glass in hand among better dressed guests. I recall my embarrasment because my water-logged shoes squeaked as I walked, and they left damp footprints on the hardwood floor.

On a recent trip to Juneau I told some local residents about my visit to the Governor's Mansion in 1958. No one would believe me. They said, "Nobody gets in there!"

Our group flew to Seattle and took another Greyhound bus homeward while Jim had taken a group of Texans from Fairbanks back down the Alcan. I never asked him, but he doubtless crossed the Peace River railroad trestle again, like a true pioneer.

For Better and for Worse

Looking back now, I recall many things over the years that may have contributed to constituting an injury to my spine, a fact that was to affect my entire life. Jumping off our porch railing onto the hard ground four feet below was a favorite trick as a child. It was something that I could do better than any of my friends. Twice my sister and I helped Father cock alfalfa hay, which is to fork the curing hay into piles, called hay cocks, with a pitchfork. Five acres of that activity made my back throb all night long. When Father got too busy to clean out the wet straw and manure from the calf pen in the barn one winter, the calves stood in muck up to their knees and were caked with manure where the body had lain in the wet bedding. I felt sorry for them, so I pitched it out and put in clean straw. I did not realize I could have removed it in thin layers, saving my strength. I worked fast and pitched out heavy forkfuls. My lower back seemed to scream in pain that night, and my father scolded me for having done this, for he knew it was much too heavy work for a growing teenage girl.

After Christmas when I was thirteen, I went *Julebukking* on skis with friends. It was a lovely winter evening until I started downhill on skis and struck a huge granite rock hidden under the surface of the snow, and this acted like brakes. I fell on my tailbone on the rock, and I literally saw stars though the sky was totally overcast. I hurt for many days after that jarring fall.

The last possible injury occurred when I was fourteen that spring. I was moving the chickenwire netting around my duckling pen, bending way over, while I pulled on a stubborn steel stake to get it out of the ground. A sudden jab of pain threw me down on the grass. This was my first major muscle spasm in the lower back, and it was a good thing I did not know then how many more of these I would experience in my lifetime! I was barely able to get into or up from a chair for many days after that. My father, out of ignorance, refused to take me to the doctor. I had no fever, was obviously not ill, and surely this would go away in time, he thought.

After about two months of repeated spasms, most not as severe as the original one, Mother insisted on taking me to the family doctor. This doctor had experienced personal back problems and surgery. Considering my not-so-bad condition, he recommended chiropractic treatments. The treatments got me over the hurdle, temporarily.

Throughout my school years until high school graduation I was excused from tumbling and certain other physical activities because I simply could not tolerate them. Chiropractic treatments helped me through the set-backs of the next 18 years. Despite major spasms at least once or twice a year, I managed to teach my own physical education classes of 5th and 6th grade pupils, running and playing with them.

On October 23, 1961, I lay resting in my bed at home thinking about these possible injuries. I had been examined by a neurosurgeon just two days before. He said that my faulty disc was too thin and poor in quality to act as a proper cushion, but it was neither a broken nor a slipped disc. He had given me the awful news that surgery was necessary.

Doing spinal fusions was yet somewhat experimental, it seemed to me, in that every neurosurgeon had a special method for handling the problem. I had expressed my fear to Dr. Christoferson over the removal of a disc in my spine, and he had put his arm around my shoulder to reassure me and had said, "If it is any consolation to you, I have removed over 3,000 discs."

I had immediately visualized a pile of 3,000 white discs heaped on the end of an operating table, and I had found that this was considerable practice on the part of the surgeon. He was also rumored to be among the seven best neurosurgeons in the world at that time. I had no choice but to ask when the surgery would be done. I was hoping to have it done at Christmas so that I could get back to work by mid-February. Little did I know what I was getting into!

"No, girl," he said. "You need this repaired at once. It has gone on far too long. I am scheduling you for surgery Tuesday morning."

Tuesday, I thought. O, God! My mother had gone through a partial removal of a disc by this same surgeon. She was fine now, but it had taken her four months to recover. I had never had any kind of surgery before, not even a tonsillectomy. I knew only that I was starting out in the major league.

I thought to myself as I lay in bed that it must be very discouraging for my husband of three months that in such a short time major surgery has to be faced. During much of our short marriage, my happiness had been marred by spells of severe pain. It was my husband's second marriage, and I was twelve years younger than he, so I'm sure he felt lucky to have found a younger wife–until all the events leading up to this day had discouraged us both. He sometimes jokingly referred to me as a broken-down model. Faulty merchandise.

My mind drifted back to our wedding day on July 16th in Oslo, Norway. John and I had spent a couple days in the home of a relative in central Norway where I reached upward to hang up a dish towel and experienced a sudden, excruciating spasm in the lower back. So it was that I had been taken to Oslo lying on a thin mattress in the back of a Ford station wagon in order to consult a kind of osteopath. His name was Odd Hagen, and he had been very sympathetic when I told him I was to be married in the Oslo Cathedral chapel in just four days!

"*Vaer ikke redd,*" (Don't be scared.) he said. "*Jeg faar deg paa foten.*" (I'll get you on your feet.) Common sense dictated that I delay our wedding. I had then thought of my poor relatives who had already purchased new hats, new purses, new neckties, and train tickets to come to our wedding. How could I let them down! I HAD to get married if I had to lie on a stretcher to do it, I decided.

Our wedding day was beautiful, and I looked fine in my royal blue suit despite rather dark circles under my eyes.

The vows had been taken, and a lady Latvian DP had sung "Jesus Saviour Pilot Me" and "The Lord's Prayer." We had turned to exit the room when we saw the caretaker of the cathedral standing in the chapel entry, wiping generous tears from his eyes. At least I have someone crying for me in my mother's absence, I thought.

My husband had seemed greatly relieved after I had recovered so quickly, I had noted. So after a four-day honeymoon in Oslo, we had headed north by train to the same home I had come from by station wagon.

Our honeymoon bed there was the same one our host and hostess had spent their honeymoon in nearly fifty years earlier. It was a tad over five feet long and about 42 inches wide, so we had slept diagonally with feet hanging over the edge. John must have suffered as much as I did, because he tried to give me the best spot in the bed. I remember he got out of the bed to sit for awhile in a chair each night to rest his tense back so that he could tolerate the bed again for a time.

That bed had been my undoing. Four days after arriving there, I had experienced another major spasm that sent me back to Oslo and Odd Hagen in the same station wagon. I had then convalesced in the home of my cousin and our best man, Leif Smestad, while my husband was flying off to London for a few days with his little boy, Dale. There was no need for them to waste John's precious vacation time sitting around waiting for me to recover.

Flying home from Norway had been extremely difficult. I had purchased a special curved orthopedic board to place behind my back to relieve the pain. After five hours on the plane I had been about to lose my sanity. An inebriated Swedish-American senior citizen from North Dakota had offered me a sample bottle of whisky on the promise that it would surely relieve the pain. He guaranteed it, he said. It was a generous offer as he had collected a large basketful of samples as souvenirs, and this was subtracting from his considerable collection.

I had never drunk whisky, but I had tasted it once or twice and so I knew why the Indians called it firewater. I was desperate for a pain killer, so I had taken the tiny bottle and swallowed the contents in one big gulp. It nearly choked me. I doubt that it killed any pain, but it definitely diverted my attention from my back to my stomach.

My husband had flown home from London at the same time as I flew home from Oslo, and we had met in Minneapolis.

Somehow I had managed to get home after that grueling trip with connecting flights and a 3-hour automobile ride.

We were at home in his house in Wahpeton, North Dakota, and I had gone back to work, teaching school for eighteen days before a severe spasm had made me an invalid again. Somehow I had recovered enough to consult my neurosurgeon, and now I lay in bed thinking about tomorrow's events. My husband would take me to a hospital in Fargo, North Dakota in the morning. I would enter the hospital where I was scheduled for a myelogram in the afternoon as a final check before surgery.

The fateful day finally came on October 25, and my back surgery went well. When I awoke, I learned the meaning of pain. For eighteen days John drove to Fargo daily from our home in Wahpeton to check on my progress and to cheer me. I was kept on so much pain killer that I wasn't aware of this big effort on his part, even though I spoke to him on each visit and was aware of his presence. I simply had no idea how many trips he was making.

Before being sent home, Dr. Christoferson who had removed the disc and Dr. Wenz who had taken bone from my hip and had ground it to create the fusion came to my room. They told me I was to wear my heavy, leather-covered steel brace night and day. It would keep me rigid from under my armpits to my mid-hip section, and it also had vertical supports on the sides and corset-like straps over the tummy.

John presented me with a size 48, pleated wool skirt to cover both me and the brace. He had shopped half the day to find one large enough.

Now I was ready to be discharged from St. John's Hospital. The girls in the office and the nurses did their last minute duties, and I was led to the elevator and put on it alone, standing on my feet (no wheelchair), while John was already in the lower level heading for our station wagon. I got down off the elevator on the proper level and waited. There were only bare walls to support me.

"Dear God, help me to hold up until John gets here with the car!" I prayed.

Suddenly, the elevator doors opened and out came the male patient from the room next to mine. He had seen me get on the elevator alone, but he had first gone to his room to pull his trousers on over his pajamas. Just as I felt I could not stand another five seconds, he had his arms around me for support.

"They sent you down here alone!" he said, incredulously. "They've gotta be crazy!"

He had a brace around the base of his neck, and it perhaps hurt him to hold me, but here he was, my savior when I needed someone. At last John backed the wagon into the garage, and the patient helped him get me into the station wagon to lie on a mattress over a sheet of plywood.

It was noon when we got home to Wahpeton, and three of the neighbor men saw us arrive and came out to help drag me on my board across the tailgate and put me into a standing position. I managed to walk the three steps up into the house and to our bedroom with John's help. Our bed stood propped up on six-inch blocks of wood, so I was able to back up to the bed and slowly roll into it. It was considerate of John to have propped up the bed, I thought.

John hired a day-time helper to care for me while he was at work. I remained in bed as I could not get into or out of bed by myself, and John trusted no one else to assist me in this.

After three days I began to vomit everything I ate. I had to lean to one side and vomit into a pail when I felt it coming on. What a miserable state I've gotten myself into, I thought! I discharged one doctor who was unable to diagnose my illness after three visits, and I got the telephone book and selected another name. Yes, they made house calls when necessary. A tall, handsome, elderly doctor called on me, and in less than three minutes he informed me that I was pregnant. By this time I had guessed as much.

How I hated to write my surgeons and inform them of this development! I had conceived shortly before I knew I had to have surgery.

Routine x-rays had to be suspended for nine months. I got stronger as time passed, and that spring I was even able to enjoy gardening by crawling around on my knees. My brace held me together, and I took it off only when I needed to get a quick sponge bath while kneeling in the tub.

Early on July 5th, I felt the first pains of labor and went to the local hospital at once. One of the first things the doctor did was to remove my back brace which I had worn night and day for nine months. It hurt a great deal simply to stand still without it! Now, with a sore and weak back that was prone to muscle spasms, I was called upon to deliver my first baby. There had been no need to hurry to the hospital because our precious, healthy daughter did not present herself until 2:17 p.m. the following day, after 30 hours of constant labor. There should be no need to explain why I decided not to have another child.

I have often reflected on how things worked out in my life. I truly did not plan any part of it. I had been like a leaf floating in a flowing stream, being carried where external influences took me. In that space of one year, I had taken a trip to Norway, gotten engaged, gotten married, adopted a stepson, acquired a new home, had major back surgery, given up my career, gotten pregnant and given birth to a lovely daughter. I truly believe I have a guardian angel.

Mindy and Family in Norwegian Sweaters, 1964

City Folk, Travelers

The twelve years I spent with my family in Wahpeton went by fast. My back slowly improved, but there were occasional setbacks due to sudden, severe muscle spasms.

Karen was a toddler of about a year and a half and about to be completely toilet trained when an unusually bad spasm put me into bed. John got me to the local osteopath for a "half treatment" which was as big a chance as the man would risk on my new fusion. I was in great pain as I stood and hung onto the table with concentration while the doctor and my husband managed to get me dressed. Somehow I got home and into bed.

John walked to his teaching job at the Wahpeton Indian School daily at 7:45 a.m., leaving me home alone with my daughter until noon when he came home for about 30 minutes. Then he would assist me to the bathroom, feed lunch to me in bed, and be gone again. A close neighbor came to assist me in the mid-afternoon, and John came home from work at 5:30.

In the middle of the day Karen played with her colored wood blocks and other toys on the living room carpet. I lay awake and listened for her whereabouts. She was admonished to stay indoors and not to answer the doorbell. Now and then she ran to my bed to talk to me and to bring a small toy to share.

When her gauze diaper was soiled, she went to the bottom drawer in the bathroom for a clean one, then scrambled onto a chair beside my bed and stood there while I reached up and changed her diaper. She dutifully took the soiled diaper by the ends and carried it to the diaper pail in the bathroom. She should have been trained being she could understand my instructions and carry out all this! On the advice of my doctor I suspended toilet training for several weeks, and this proved to be good advice.

When Karen grew weary and needed a nap, she crawled up onto a chair and got into the crib by herself. When she awakened, she managed to crawl out from the crib and get down. It was more like a baby sitting an adult than an adult sitting a baby.

I kept a garden those years in which I raised some vegetables and lots of flowers. We had planted flowering crabs, an apple tree, a snowball bush, and many tulips. We had every reason to be proud of our back yard.

The children had to be taken to the city park for swimming

lessons every summer and to the ice rink for skating in the winter. There were Cub Scout meetings for Dale and Brownies and 4-H activities for Karen. I gave piano lessons to both and taught Sunday School.

Our family took a vacation trip every summer because John had vacation time annually. We visited places like Rocky Mountain National Park, Glacier and Yellowstone National Parks, The Grand Tetons, a 4th of July rodeo at Red Lodge, Montana, and the Black Hills. We also visited the Shepherd of the Hills country in the Ozarks three summers, and we took in the Land of Lincoln and Hannibal and St. Louis, Missouri.

In 1968, after saving money from renting out rooms to tech school students for several years, we planned for a summer in Europe. John had been accepted to attend the International Summer School in Oslo, Norway, as I had in 1955, and I was excited about showing Karen what Norway, the land of her ancestors, was like.

Karen and I flew to New York City on May 3 and changed terminals at Kennedy International Airport to get an SAS plane to Oslo's Fornebu Airport the next day. Karen was big-eyed to see the lights of New York City grow smaller as we rose higher into the night, and she was equally excited over the snow-covered mountains around Bergen as seen from the air. She was even more excited to suddenly come out from under the cloud layer west of Oslo to discover farm animals, cars, and people moving around the very green countryside as we were about to land. It looked like an exciting place.

We got rid of jet lag by staying in Oslo two nights with friends and seeing the sights on foot before taking a train to Fagernes in Valdres in central Norway, four hours to the north.

We spent a week there visiting the farm home of my grandparents who had left Norway for America in 1883, the Volbu Church of my ancestors, and many families who were relatives. To me, it was like coming home as this was my fourth trip to Norway.

While there, it snowed one night, dumping about six inches of the wet stuff. Karen and I were thrilled to put on our plastic rain boots and walk around on the country roads enjoying this winter version of Norway. Low clouds and some morning fog obscured the tops of the mountains.

We took the train back to Oslo after nearly a week in the Valdres Valley. There we got on a first class sleeping car to Copenhagen for $5.90. We arrived refreshed the next morning and found ourselves next door to the famous Tivoli Park as we left the train station. Trees already wore big green leaves here, and there were tulips in bloom everywhere. We took a cab to our hotel which turned out to be only four blocks from the station. John and Dale would meet us at this hotel in a day and a half. We spent the afternoon in Tivoli Park where Karen enjoyed the carrousel rides and the Lego train. There was plenty of sightseeing left over for the next day, too. She can remember climbing up on the Hans Christian Anderson statue.

When John and Dale pulled up under our window in a cab, we ran down stairs to greet them. Almost the first thing John told me was that he had lost his travelers checks and had very little money. The checks in fact were still at home somewhere. He had discovered this while in New York and had called back to Linda, our neighbor, who had a key to our house. She had gone through every drawer and shelf in our home without finding them, and she had also searched his desk at the Indian School where he taught. No travelers checks. Fortunately for all of us, I had taken extra emergency money with me and had prepaid most of our hotel rooms. We set out to see the continent for one month on a Eurrail Pass and my emergency money.

Every day had its highlight. We saw Copenhagen with John and Dale before crossing Denmark and much of the Netherlands. Amsterdam and the Anne Frank house were very special as were Volendam and the Isle of Marken. We enjoyed the boat trip down Hans Brinker's canal to Broek in Holstein cow and Edom cheese country.

The soaring Cologne Cathedral dwarfed us as we stepped off the train beside it. There was a new bridge over the Rhine River behind the cathedral and a huge shopping area with a walking mall out front that covered the area that was piled up rubble from World War II when I had last seen it in 1953.

We took a boat down the Rhine, decorated with castles, to Mainz where we got off the train to marvel at the Gutenberg Bible and the Gutenberg printing press as well as the illuminated pages of the Bibles hand copied by monks long ago.

The next stop was Heidelberg where Karen and I bought two small Hummel figurines for $6 each. These sell for over $130 today. John and Dale walked through the famous castle there which I had visited before.

The Black Forest was a fairy land, especially Triberg, nestled among the evergreen-covered hills. We climbed along its Gutach Falls and enjoyed the squirrels with their tall, tufted ears. Cuckoo clocks ticked in all the shops. Our two huge bedrooms and two huge sitting rooms in the Löwen-Schwarzwald Hotel for $6 per night for the entire family was the most fantastic of all!

The pastel city of Lucerne lay serenely before us. One did not ever want to leave such a lovely place. We took a dizzying ride on a cable car to the summit of Mt. Pilatus, and the view of the famous peaks of Switzerland from up there was quite fantastic. We enjoyed throwing some snowballs before we had to leave for a descent on the funicular.

The next day we made our way to Liechtenstein. The entire country was visible with one scan of the eyes, and we walked among the finest vineyards in Vaduz that I had ever seen.

After Garmisch, Oberammergau, Wies Church, and Neuschwanstein Castle we spent some time in Salzburg and Innsbruck. Mozart's home in Salzburg was of great interest to Karen, a budding pianist. Our hotel, the Schwarzes Rossel (the Black Horse), was memorable because all the furniture in our room was of hand-carved wood, and the feather tickings on the beds were so full and piled so high that Karen almost sank out of sight in them.

Our hotel in Innsbruck had been there when Columbus sailed for America! Gasthoff Innsbruche, a skinny pink hotel, had an original staircase post still in use dated 1425! Of course the hotel had been remodeled a number of times, but the post truly looked that old.

A long, dark tunnel through Brenner Pass soon took us to Venice. The children remember the Italian spaghetti, the continental rolls, and all that Venetian glass better than the scenery. Karen will never forget having seven pigeons on her head and shoulders at the same time. We stayed in Hotel Concordia right beside the Cathedral of St. Mark, and we had a private, close-up view of the upper level of the Cathedral.

Enroute to Florence a friendly train conductor named Antonio enjoyed communicating with Karen who was soon six, and he enjoyed showing off her drawings of cowboys on horses to other conductors.

After the numerous sights of Rome we took a *rapido treno* to Genoa. Karen still remembers the six-room private hotel we stayed in with a view of the Medieval gates in the ancient wall that surrounds the city and the remains of the house that is believed to be the home of Christopher Columbus . But a most unusual event had just happened before we walked into the hotel. We rang the bell at the desk for service, and the manager appeared in a distant doorway and waved us an invitation to come to a tiny room. There we found about nine people sitting with tear-stained faces watching television. A news report was on. We were given chairs to sit on. Robert Kennedy had just been assassinated. This Italian family and their friends were saddened and emotional over this happening. Only when the report was over would they take our reservation slip and show us to our room. This moment of intimate and mutual concern with this Italian family is unforgettable.

One has not seen a cathedral until one has seen the Milan Duomo! It is a huge Gothic structure built like a massive cake with hundreds of larger-than-life-size statues that decorate it like fancy icing on a fancy cake. Inside are 52 huge pillars, well-spaced, for 52 weeks in a year. Floor to ceiling is 200 feet. We found the entrance to the elevator that took us to the roof, and we walked around up there on stone slabs that had become worn down in the centers from the feet of perhaps millions of tourists through the decades, even the centuries. It gave us a great view of the cathedral and the city, and we hated to have to come down again.

Seeing Leonardo Da Vinci's painting of "The Last Supper" was a thrill. It is much more beautiful than it appears in the reproductions. It is painted on a wall in the dining hall of the Santa Maria delle Grazie Monastery, the roof and other three walls of which were destroyed during World War II. A miracle seems to have preserved it for us.

Our stay at Stresa on the shore of Lake Maggiore in northern Italy was wonderful, but we had to press on to Oslo. We left in a night train sleeper from Milan, and we slept just fine except for the passport interruptions by the conductors.

The next morning we awakened in time to stick our heads out the train window to see our entire train going onto a ferry boat that would take us into Denmark and Copenhagen. It was Saturday, and the lost travelers checks still had not been reissued. The office was closed on Saturdays, so John had to stay behind and go to the office early Monday morning. We three left him there and took the train to Oslo and a hotel. He came to Oslo Monday noon on a plane.

Summer school lasted six weeks, and it took John to Finland and Sweden for field trips as well as into the mountains for skiing and a bit of walking on glaciers. Dale went to live with relatives on the west coast where he caught such a huge cod in the North Sea that the relatives are still talking about it. Karen and I stayed in Bjørknes Skole, a private high school, as guests of Alice Bjørknes. We slept on beds in a classroom and cooked on a tiny electric plate. We went everywhere in Oslo that our feet and the streetcars could take us. One day we walked down to the docks to see the *M.S.Oslofjord* passenger ship in dock. John and I had made our first trans-Atlantic crossing on that. We sometimes visited museums and sometimes parks. We went bathing in Sognsvaten at the end of the streetcar line, and we enjoyed shopping.

Before John's classes started, we took a train to Bergen and got a room in a private home because hotels were filled. The aquarium is one of our favorite places there with its comical penguins and wonderful close-up views of marine life. We enjoyed the flower and fish market where the goods are fresh daily, and of course we took the funicular to the top of Fløyen for a fantastic view of Bergen. Then it was time to take a hydrofoil boat to the island of Bømlo from where John's parents had come when they immigrated to North Dakota.

This was my first trip to meet John's first cousins, and they had not seen Karen before, either. Their dialect took a bit of getting used to, but we understood one another rather well. We stayed in the home of three single siblings in their middle-age years: Alma, Martha, and Peter. They were to become favorites of all of us. They had a lively interest in us and in America, and their sense of humor was terrific. Karen and I didn't know it then, but their home would be considered home to both of us henceforth.

Relatives took us to Moster Church that Grandma Elizabeth had talked about so often. It was here the Viking, Olaf Tryggvason, had landed when he returned from England in 1000 A.D. after becoming a Christian. Here he had ordered a church to be built, and here it still stood, the oldest church structure in Norway today. We tried out the old blue wooden pews and the stalls where children were kept who were to be baptised that Sunday. We marveled at the stall for "unclean" women after giving birth–where they had to sit in humiliation for a certain number of weeks until they were permitted to return to their regular seats. We climbed to check out the bell in the tower.

We were taken to the farm homes of Grandma Elizabeth and Grandpa Peder Andreas and to the Bremnes Church in which they had been baptised and confirmed. Bremnes Church would be 100 years old in a few months and was newly restored and painted in excellent taste in shades of grays and white with farmer-red pews and red carpet down the aisle. From the church one can see the Gaasland farm across a water body.

Many days were spent with relatives in their cozy homes. Norwegians have a tradition of serving guests graciously and attractively. Their home is their castle, and what goes on the table by way of dishes and tableware is just as important as the food. They make their guests seem special by the way every meal and snack is served.

Nils Stautland was also a notable relative in that he would later marry and take his family to America to visit us twice. He was also on hand to drive us around and entertain us on each successive trip. John has fished in the North Sea with him more than once.

The time came all too soon to get on the Bergensbanen back to Oslo. This is a beautiful trip of about eight hours through snow-capped mountains, past glaciers and permanently frozen lakes.

When Karen and I tired of walking all over Oslo, we took the train back to our relatives in Valdres and were greeted warmly there. We had many homes to stay in. We even stayed on the seter or summer pastures above the timberline in the mountains. Here Karen played with the milk goats from which the milk comes for making the famous *gjetost* or goat cheese. The goats were real pests, attempting to eat the very buttons off her coat. But she was already a farm girl at heart and managed to let them out of their pen in the morning and to help enclose them at night. There was also an adorable striped kitten to play with, and relatives took her fishing in a high mountain lake.

Last of all we enjoyed staying on the Eivind Mattisgaard farm from which my grandparents had emmigrated. My second cousin and his family lived simply and expected us to make ourselves at home, which we did. Their Berit was Karen's age, and her two little brothers were little rascals. They tied their father's neckties together to tie the door handle to a bed post to keep out their mother. Those were lively days for Karen.

We joined John back in Oslo, and when his physical education classes took to the mountains in western Norway, Karen and I traveled by bus and kept pace with them. All four of us revisited Valdres before flying to London for a short visit.

August 20th found us back in our home at Wahpeton. The lost travelers checks turned up unexpectedly three days later when I grabbed a dirty white shirt from our closet shelf, intending to throw it into the washing machine. It had the checks wrapped inside. My husband, who always thinks I am foolish to lock the door, had hidden the checks so well that he could not recall where he had put them. Would he return them to the bank? No, he sent his wife to do that.

We Go Farming

John retired from 25 years of teaching Native American children in 1972. In anticipation of this event we had purchased a medium-sized farm close to Glenwood, Minnesota, in 1968. Now we could make plans to move there. First, the old house needed to be torn down and removed, and a new house had to be built.

John's and Mindy's Pope County Farm

John tore down the part wood, part double brick structure by himself using a chain saw, heavy chains, and an old farm tractor. It's amazing he survived this dangerous task. He then hired two carpenters and went to work on a new house in the fall of 1972 and winter of 1973. Karen and I stayed in Wahpeton where she completed the 5th grade. Dale was off to college and a career of his own, so he never lived on this farm.

In the spring of 1973, John moved his herd of registered Hereford cows onto the farm from his ranch in North Dakota which he had sold. We had just hired two men to put up miles of new barbed-wire fence. We were both farm-raised, and he knew beef cattle whereas I was more familiar with dairy cattle. But knowing is a bit different from doing.

The cows calved in April and May, and we lost four of our first crop of calves. All died during the birth process, so that was not a good record. Some had to be pulled into the world. John went to a neighbor and bought replacement Holstein dairy calves. He got the cows to accept them as their own by putting the cow into the cattle chute and letting the calf go to her to nurse. It took some cows several days to accept the new calf.

John hired three watering holes blasted out in the pasture. The neighbors thought he was crazy, but he used this North Dakota method. The cattle could not be expected to walk one to two miles up and down hills twice a day just to get a drink.

Meanwhile, we moved our household things into the new house in the deep mud of spring, but moving and settling into the house was the easy part of my work to be done that summer. I had to pick up a truck load of tin cans and other garbage that generations of tenants had heaved into the woods near the house. I helped John pull down 65 scraggly boxelder trees that grew close together like weeds on the yard. We selected and saved the best trees, notably one beautiful, huge bur oak. Then I raked piles of dirt into place to create and seed a level lawn. This I watered morning and evening. I also created a garden from a cleared area near a former chicken house. There the manure could be found straight down to China! The squash I grew there that summer were the largest I have ever seen.

I was baking cookies one June day and admiring my newly-created lawn from the kitchen window when suddenly the four Holstein calves turned up out of nowhere and sprinted across the tender grass and soft earth. They were followed by my husband who trotted after them, not being able to overtake them or herd them toward the pen. They all stomped around in circles.

I dropped my work and ran out toward the calves with my right hand held out toward them, palm side up. The calf closest to me listened to my cooing sounds and came and began sucking on my fingers as I slowly walked backwards into the pen beside the barn. The calf did not let go, but kept pace with me, and the others followed. I shut the gate.

John came over with a puzzled look on his face, scratched his head and said, "Where did you learn that trick?"

Hereford calves will not do this. In fact, it's not easy to teach them to drink from a pail, either. A Holstein sucks eagerly on one's fingers, so by lowering the hand slowly into a pail of warm milk, the calf is suddenly sucking the milk. It's a piece of cake.

I had to learn to walk, not run, after the cattle when they got out. John handled them calmly. I also discovered it wasn't necessary to round up the very last cow. Get the lead cows and most of the herd headed in the right direction and the stragglers will follow and eventually catch up.

John had a full-time job as a farmer, and our main crop was hay. We took two and sometimes three cuttings in the warm season. At first we baled all the alfalfa and native grass into rectangular bales. No more cutting with a short-swath mower, raking it into windrows with a horse-drawn rake, and cocking the hay by hand. No more loading loose hay onto a hay rack with a pitchfork, then pulling it to the track in the roof of the big Gothic-roof barn with rope slings pulled by a single horse as my father had done.

We had a new haybine which cut and crimped the hay and left it in neat rows. When cured, John hired a highschool boy to stand on the hayrack, pulled behind the baler, to grab the bales from the baler. John drove the tractor slowly, and the boy stacked each bale on the rack until they had a load. Then they drove home to unload, one bale at a time, onto an elevator that took the bales to the haymow. Here they were dropped at random, but here John stacked them as they came off the elevator. No rain spoiled this hay.

A few years later, around 1980, we went to big round bales. Then the whole operation required only one man, John.

There's always some spoilage on the bale exterior from rain and mold, especially if the ground is very wet . I suggested to John that he try putting some of the fresh bales into the huge white barn that sheltered the cattle in winter storms, then remove them when it got cold in the fall, thus keeping them rain-free. It took him two years to consider my suggestion. After the first experimental storage he did this every year. It meant moving the bales twice, but there was no wasted, spoiled hay.

Marketing was also experimental at first. We soon learned that sending cattle to South St. Paul was traditional around Glenwood. It is a good market for old Holstein cows and Holstein steers, but it is not a good market for beef calves. We tried three places before settling on the Sisseton, South Dakota salesbarn. Our cattle frequently topped the market there. It took a few years, but eventually most beef farmers around Glenwood sent their calves to Sisseton.

John tried raising purebred bulls. They just didn't sell well here. But one incident helped him to decide suddenly to quit raising bulls. We had a nice, 12-foot soft maple that we had moved from Wahpeton to our yard on the farm. The bulls were penned when we left home, but when we came home two hours later at dusk, they were on the yard stomping holes in the lawn.

Just after we got them chased back into the pen with our Bonnie's help, we discovered our soft maple tree lying on the ground. It had a crotch in it, and a bull had walked right through that crotch, splitting the tree. One half fell to the east, one to the west.

The next morning I wanted John to cut it to the ground. He went for a ladder, some rope, and an auger instead. We struggled to raise the two parts and tie them together. Then he found six lag bolts, drilled the holes in the tree, and bolted it together.

About fifteen years later, the tree would be huge and gorgeous in the fall in its golden leaves. Only he who someday fells the tree and hits the bolts with his chainsaw will know where the bolts are.

John bought two dapple-grey Arabian foals that first spring. We named the mare Greygo and the gelding Silver. Karen and John trained them together with patient persistence for they were very lively.

One sultry summer night after a week of rain, I awakened to the sound of thundering hooves. Were they cattle? Horses? I sprang from my bed to the windows. I saw Greygo in the yard light heading for my new flowering crab and rubbing the mosquitos off as she brushed by it. I glimpsed Silver stomping across the lawn, leaving holes.

"John! Wake up!" I shouted. "Horses!"

"What?" John asked irritably.

"Horses are loose on the yard! Hurry!" I demanded.

I was into my shoes in seconds and grabbed the broom on the way out. I ran to open the gate by the barn, but it was already open. This is where they got out, I thought. Then John came and chased the horses toward the pen, and in no time they were corralled with the gate shut. It was very dark out, but as I turned, John walked into the circle of light made by the yard light. He wore his slippers, but he didn't have on one stitch of clothing!

"You are running around out here stark naked!" I scolded incredulously. "What if someone should drive into the yard!"

"Who the heck is going to drive into the yard at 3 o'clock in the morning!" he answered.

Who indeed? I looked down at myself. I was in my baby-doll pajamas.

We went into the house and tried to sleep another three hours, but I dozed and then dreamed of hearing thundering hooves. At 6:30 I went out and got black dirt and filled in the holes that the horses had made. I hated nothing more than having my beautiful lawn damaged by animals.

Hereford Cow with Twin Calves

Karen was in the sixth grade that first term on the farm. She joined Lakeview 4-H Club and was very active. In the ensuing years she won lots of ribbons and awards, but her two greatest thrills were winning a trophy on her Arabian mare, Greygo, for halter class at our County Fair and winning a week's trip to the National 4-H Club Congress in Chicago as Minnesota State Champion in Veterinary Science. The week was spent in the Hilton Hotel, formerly Stevens Hotel, the world's largest at that time.

Karen also took piano lessons every year, and she enjoyed flute lessons while in high school. She went off to college after high school graduation but always enjoyed coming home to the horses, dogs and cats.

We had our cow-calf operation for nineteen and a half years before selling the herd and moving to town. These were happy years, although years of long days and hard work. Many strange and sad things happened here as well as funny and wonderful things.

The following stories tell of special experiences we had while on this farm.

Our Red Barn

Karen Learns Horsemanship

Karen's first pony was a mixed-breed mare, part Welch pony and part Shetland. The mare was a dark buckskin, so she named her Cinnamon. Karen was then twelve years old.

Cinnamon's confidence was soon won over as Karen rode her. But ponies are not known for a smooth gait, and Karen looked forward to riding a full-sized horse.

She coaxed Cinnamon uphill in the cattle lane one summer's day, heading for the open pasture. Cinnamon, as usual, fought the whole way to go back to the barn. At the end of the cattle lane, Karen turned Cinnamon around to go home. The cattle lane had trees and some small bushes on the south side, open space on the north side. As they headed east toward home, Cinnamon needed no urging. But why she suddenly darted into the trees rather than staying out in the open, only Cinnamon knew.

I had come to the gate where the lane starts, to watch Karen ride. I could see that Cinnamon was gaining speed, and suddenly, she came to a fallen tree trunk with a small brush pile on the other side. Karen later said that she was prepared for Cinnamon to swerve before coming to the tree, but instead, the little mare made one mighty leap over both obstacles. Karen got jolted out of the saddle and came down on Cinnamon's neck in front of the saddle horn. Still holding the reins and her feet still in the stirrups, Karen clung to the pony's neck, desperately trying not to fall off Cinnamon.

Cinnamon tore right through some low branches, and I feared broken eye glasses would injure Karen's eyes as I yelled, "Karen! Watch out for your glasses!"

At that point, Karen was in no position to do anything about her glasses, and to this day she thinks I was more concerned for the cost of breaking her glasses than for her personal safety.

Somehow Karen hung on all the way to the barn door in this jiggling, painful position. She had learned that she was not in control of her pony and that there remained a lot to learn about horsemanship.

Several years later she had learned to ride rather well. She sometimes rode Greygo or Silver, our Arabians, all over the farm. One day she took Silver and told me she was riding to the farthest west pasture, and she would be home in one hour or so. She loved to ride out there where she could observe deer and fox, woodchucks and Canada geese and get close to them on horseback.

I was mowing our big lawn with our sixteen-horsepower riding mower when she left on Silver.

Some forty minutes later Silver appeared at the gate, heading for the barn. He still wore the saddle, but the reins hung down and he was stumbling on them as he trotted. Worse, he was sweaty and foamy-white with lather. A vision of my daughter being dragged to her death by this runaway horse terrified me just as John came to the gate driving his pickup. I had by now turned off the mower motor and jumped off the lawn mower. I pointed to Silver and shouted to John, "Go find Karen!"

In a glance toward Silver he comprehended the situation, stepped on the gas, and tore up the cattle lane.

I prayed aloud for Karen's safety as I walked slowly toward Silver with grass in my hand. I managed to grab the reins and put him into the barn.

I ran toward the gate, but before I got there, John was back with the pickup. Seated beside him was a smiling Karen. Smiling and unhurt but disgusted. Only a mother can appreciate the relief I felt!

Silver, I might have known, had untied the reins from the tree where Karen had tied him when she went to investigate a new-born calf. The harder she tried to approach him, the faster he stumbled along toward home. Silver could take halters off other horses and open chained gates–a real Houdini-type horse!

Pegleg Pete

We discovered during our first two summers on the farm that we knew much less about farming than we had thought. John knew a lot about Hereford cattle, but he had not been in the role of farmer for many years.

John stuck his head inside the kitchen doorway one May afternoon at about 5:30 and said that he was going to the far west pasture to check on the cows. This was our second summer on the farm, and our pregnant heifers as well as the older cows still calved in the pasture.

"I'll be home for supper about 6:20," he said, and then he left.

It was over a mile out there, so I knew better than to expect him back before 7:00. Karen and I delayed eating until 7:30, and when 8:00 o'clock rolled around, he still had not come home. At 9:00 there was no John, either. I began to get very worried. Had he tippped the tractor? Drowned in a waterhole? Been gored by a cow?

I suggested to Karen who was just 13 now that I had better go to check on him. I delayed action as I knew she didn't like being home by herself in the evenings. By 10:00 she was ready to go to bed, and I told her to lock the doors while I drove the car to look for him. I put on old bluejeans and a jacket, grabbed the big lantern, and headed for the door. As I opened it I met John in the doorway looking dirty and very wet and all of ten years older!

Before I could ask a single question he ordered me to come at once to the barn. "Get old clothes on," he said. "A heifer is trying to calf, and she needs help. I've chased her all over creation, but I've got her in the barn now. Hurry!" With that he disappeared into the darkness.

Karen had heard what he said, so she went to bed, somewhat relieved.

I already had old clothes on, and I followed him out, lantern in hand. Thankfully, we had electric lights in the old barn.

I could see this heifer was smaller than most. The calf's front feet were protruding, and her waterbag had broken. She had been running this way for over an hour. John told me he had tried to tie her to a tree in the pasture, but she had gotten wild and broken away.

He worked fast to adjust the calf-puller over her hips and struggled to hook the chain around the hooves of the calf. He said he had chased her about an eighth of a mile toward home when she bolted and turned back to stand in the farthest waterhole. There she remained no matter how many stones John threw at her or how much he yelled at her. So, he took off his shoes and jeans and waded in after her. Not wanting to swim in any deeper water, she came out. Then he had to get his clothes on and chase her toward home. This was repeated for the second and third waterholes. He had chased her for over a mile, much of it backtracking and uphill.

Now he ordered me to crank the calf-puller. I knelt behind the cow and cranked with all my strength while John grabbed the feet and pulled. I thought we had failed when suddenly the huge bull calf almost shot into my lap. The poor heifer's ordeal was over.

We dragged the calf around to lie in front of her head and left them alone. John went into the house to clean up and eat some cold supper.

At 5:00 a.m. we found an alert, clean calf with the mother standing over him. To our surprise, the calf had not nursed. John pulled him to his feet, but the calf fell when he let go. One front leg and shoulder seemed to sag, and he could not stand on that leg. We had pulled something too hard.

John had to put the cow into the chute and milk her. I ran to the house for the plastic bag with an attached feeding hose. We filled it with her warm milk, and John straddled the frisky calf and force-fed him. In minutes, he got the hang of it and sucked greedily. We then changed to a nipple bottle.

A day later he still couldn't stand. I got an idea. "Let's try putting a splint on his leg," I suggested.

John asked in a scoffing tone, "Just how do you plan to do that?"

"Get some sturdy but slim wood strips," I said. "I'll get an old sheet and pad his leg. Then we'll tape the wood strips along his leg."

He didn't argue. We had to try something.

When it was finished, the calf was propped up, and to our surprise he stayed on his feet. But it took a couple days before he learned to lie down and get up again by himself with his stiff, burdened leg. We had to give him milk replacer in water and dry up his mother. She soon returned to grazing, and then we had to teach him to drink from a pail. He would bunt the pail when it got nearly empty and pivot around on his pegleg. I dubbed him Pegleg Pete.

He was a large, greedy calf who, after some days, got a bad case of diarrhea. We cut down on his food and gave him more water, and the problem cleared up. By that time he had lost the hair from around his anus from the runny excrement. Medicated salve applied to the area daily helped clear it up.

A veterinarian came to the farm for another animal two weeks after Pegleg was born. He noted the splint on the calf who by now was pivoting in circles around his wooden leg and was getting up and down with ease. The vet heard the whole story and took the splint off. Much to his surprise, Pegleg Pete was totally healed and could run like a proper calf.

A day or two later, Karen felt sorry for him being penned in the barn in the shade when other calves were outdoors in the sun. She found rope and tied him outside the barn door in the sun. The sun was very intense on his bare bottom where the hair had not yet grown back, and he was outside in the sun too long. The next day he had a red rash and watery blisters there. More medicated salve was used, and it took two weeks to heal properly.

Pegleg Pete was growing and filling out very well. He had great conformation, and he looked like the picture of health. He would make a great herd bull yet.

Two high school boys came to help John bale and haul hay one July day. That day the temperature reached 98 degrees with a humidity to match. At noon the guys sat shirtless at the kitchen table, sweating so profusely that I gave each of them a big towel to wipe off their steaming bodies. At 2:00 p.m. it had become unbearable, so John discharged his helpers for the day.

We sat down a minute or two to talk and rest. Suddenly, at the same time, each of us remembered Pegleg Pete in the barn. He had been given nothing to drink since 7:30 a.m.

"I don't suppose anyone remembered to give Pegleg Pete water at noon," John said looking accusingly at me. We ran to the barn with water, but Pegleg Pete was lying prone in the straw, his tongue protruding. My feet flew back to the house for the nipple bottle which I filled with warm water and milk.

Pegleg Pete tried, but he was too exhausted to swallow. He died in John's arms of heat and dehydration. He was a great calf who didn't get enough of a chance. Win a few, lose a few–that's farming.

The Great Duck Roundup

Raising ducklings had been my special joy in growing up, and I wanted to give our daughter that experience, too. She was enthusiastic about all animals and birds on the farm. We had already raised fifty Indian River heavy hens, and we kept a few Buff Orpingtons, Barred Rocks and Rhode Island Reds–our favorite chickens. We saw an ad in the local paper for white Pekin ducks on a farm near Forada. John, Karen and I drove out to look. They were fine-looking, pure Pekins, so we purchased three hens and a drake. On another place that the seller recommended, we were able to trade the drake for one unrelated to Karen's hens.

Karen enjoyed the whole project just as I had. She collected the eggs as they were laid in the duck pen in the barn, and when she had enough for a hatch, about ten eggs, she put them under a broody chicken hen that farmers refer to as a "setting hen." Four broody hens incubated the duck eggs in 28 days, a week longer than chicken eggs require. The newly-hatched ducklings, little balls of yellow fluff, were transferred to a tiny house and round pen about 20 feet in diameter out on green grass. The hens clucked and fussed over them as they ate wet mash and waded into their water pan. They must have thought their chicks were strange to like slopping in water!

In just a few weeks the ducklings were fast outgrowing their need for their mother hens, but they did enjoy huddling with their heads under their mothers' feathers at night.

When the ducklings grew adult feathers, we decided to let them go into the slough by day. Then the mother hens really got excited as they had to stay on shore for hours, calling to the ducklings. But they always returned to the hens when they grew weary or when Karen called for them to get their food and penned them in for the night.

Meanwhile, the three duck hens quit laying. Or so we thought. Unknown to us, one hen had laid a few eggs in a depression among the cattails. When her first duckling hatched out, she abandoned the rest of her eggs. The mother duck wanted to keep company with the other adult ducks, and the little duckling got left behind one day.

Karen felt sorry for him out there alone, and he would surely die without his mother's care. Karen managed to catch the duckling and brought him into our house to put him into an empty apple carton, the kind that has six quarter-sized holes along the sides. Here he lay on clean newspapers and a rag for a bed. He ate and drank and soiled his paper floor while he observed me as he peeked with one eye out one of the holes. I spoke to him as I worked, and he "quackled" back at me. He was otherwise quiet.

He slept for long stretches of time, but when I left the kitchen, he would peek through the holes and quack loudly. As soon as I came back to the kitchen, all was quiet.

He soon went to live in the barn where we found another broody chicken who adopted him. Karen made a real pet of him, and he learned to come when called and to eat from her hand.

We had been correct in calling the duckling "he" early on, as he was becoming a large, handsome drake. It was the summer of the Watergate scandal, so Karen named him Tricky Dicky. He had outgrown his surrogate mother and was fully feathered when Karen decided to let him join the thirty-some older ducks in the slough. He happily took to water and swam after the others.

To our great dismay they did not welcome him but swam away from him to the opposite shore. Tricky Dicky swam gamely after, but he looked like a sinking submarine. His body definitely was not out of water far enough to swim well. Then we realized that his chicken mother had not taught him to preen his feathers properly. He was sinking for lack of oil in his feathers. We watched helplessly.

On the far side of the pond, the ducks waded on shore and lay down to rest. It took Tricky Dicky another ten minutes to get on shore, too, and he was kept away from the others by their jabbing at him with their bills when he came close. But he was undaunted. He was, after all, a cut larger than the other drakes. He began to work with his wet feathers. He stood there and preened for a good half hour.

White Pekin Ducks, Tricky Dicky in Center

Later that afternoon, Karen called him home to get food. By then he was swimming well. The entire flock waddled up on dry land, but only Tricky Dicky came and ate from Karen's hand. The other jealous ducks waited in awe of his bravery.

Tricky Dicky gradually became wild like the others. By October none of them would come to land when Karen called. They were to be butchered for eating, and they could not be out in the slough when it got below freezing.

We wasted many hours on attempts to lure them to shore and get them penned. All attempts failed. At last our son, Dale, and his wife, Peggy, came to visit. They kept a canoe in our machine shed.

We decided to try having Dale and Peggy paddle the canoe out to chase them home. We extended the sides of the chicken-wire pen way into the cattails and tramped down a swath of cattails, creating a makeshift path to the pen.

It worked–almost. All but three got corralled. Karen and I waded and stumbled around among six-foot cattails to run down these last few ducks. Fortunately, they stumbled and got their feet caught in cattails, too, and it helped that they wanted to head for their quacking comrades instead of the water. I caught them one by one. The great duck roundup was complete. We could no longer tell which drake was Tricky Dicky.

No Easter Joy in the Barn

A neighbor had borrowed our cattle chute and brought it back very dirty. We don't know if this is where the disease came from, but suddenly one new calf after the other began to sicken and die within one or two days.

We'd had a few good calf crops, but this one was proving to be a disaster. After losing four calves outside, John decided to put the cows that were closest to calving into the barn to isolate them from the others. He had consulted our veterinarian, but at this point we did not have a proper diagnosis. This was done on Good Friday afternoon, and by Saturday afternoon there were four new calves.

Early the next morning I went to the barn to feed the cats. John was still asleep. I put on a light and walked in. I saw the four calves from yesterday and two new ones, just born and being washed off. The four day-old ones looked very strange. All were lying down, looking listless, but there was something else. Their eyes looked dry and sunken. Yes, one calf's eyes were sinking right back into its head!

The cows stood with full udders. I knew then that these four calves would die. In fact, the one was dying right then.

I tore back to the house and awakened John. He was soon out there to see for himself. He decided to further isolate the two that had been born during the night, so they were put into another barn with their mothers. I felt sick in the pit of my stomach. Sick to see beautiful, healthy-looking calves begin to sicken and die, even before their naval cords had shriveled.

John called the vet who came in a half-hour. This time the vet saw the tragedy unfold before his eyes. He believed it to be a bovine diarrhea, so he informed us that all new calves had to be vaccinated before they were three hours old. He would call for the vaccine. Before he had gone, we could see symptoms in one of the two born during the night. The next day all six were dead. None were born that night, and later Monday morning we acquired the vaccine. Now we had to watch night and day for new calves to get the vaccine into their mouths as soon as possible after birth. Once we began vaccinating, no more calves died. We vaccinated every year after that.

I will never forget the sinking, helpless feeling of dread I had when I realized those calves were dying. I felt sorry for my husband who was so proud of his herd and who worked very hard to make everything go right. It wasn't so much the money we were losing as the struggle for life we were losing.

I felt pity for the mooing cows who could not understand why their sick calves did not respond and get up and nurse. It was plain to see their unwillingness to accept death as they smelled of their dying calves. They seemed to have feelings that go beyond wanting to be nursed dry. Even after they had been turned out for several days, some cows came back to the barn bellowing and listening and waiting.

Thank God for vaccine! Had we known sooner what to do, we could have spared the animals and ourselves much misery.

Mindy Conquers Hypothermia

John had been getting up in the middle of the night for nearly a week to check on his pregnant cows and had concluded that they were not going to calf within the next few days. That last night he had slept straight through to 6:00 a.m. when he got up to get an early start to drive to Grand Forks to visit his hospitalized brother, Arne.

"Don't worry, none of the cows are quite ready to calf," he said when I asked what I was to do in that case.

Before he got into the car, I spotted a white blob up by the big white barn.

"What's that lying up by the white barn?" I asked. "It looks like a calf."

"Impossible. I told you not to worry about calving," he said.

Just then I noticed that a cow was standing near the blob, and she turned to look at it.

"Look," I said, "that cow standing close to it looks awfully interested in that blob. Maybe it's her calf."

John still was not convinced, but the cow moved closer to the white blob. It was too far away to be seen clearly.

"You could at least walk up there and check it out before you leave," I said rather impatiently.

John had wanted an early start, and going up to check would take at least ten minutes. If it should be a calf at least a half hour could be lost. He grudgingly walked up to look. It had dipped down to 27 degrees that April night, and he soon saw that I was right. What he found was a hypothermic calf lying prone on its side.

It was a huge bull calf, and it was lying on the wrong side of the fence. Evidently the mother had been lying with her rear toward the fence when she gave birth, and the calf had slid out under the barbed wire so that she could not lick him dry. The temperature was not that bad that birthing would otherwise have been a problem. The calf's size also contributed to his just lying there rather than attempting to get up and nurse quickly. He may have been born very early in the night.

John had to come back to the machine shed where he found a big canvas to place the calf on, and then he pulled him down the hill over the thin layer of snow and managed to get him into the barn. The cow followed, so it was not difficult to get her in. He had managed to do this without getting so dirty that he had to change clothes, but he went into the house and washed his hands.

"You'll have to take a pail of real warm water down to him and start washing him to see if you can get life back into him," he said. He had little faith in that calf being able to live, and he knew that I knew no more about what to do than he did. "I've got to get going," he said, and he left. It was 7:30 a.m.

I had eaten my breakfast, so I put on warmer clothing and took a pail of very warm water and a rag and headed for the barn. I washed the prone calf on the one side for about fifteen minutes, running back to the house twice for more warm water. Then with a mighty effort on my part, I managed to turn him over, and I repeated the process. I had brought out several badly worn bath towels from the house and used them to rub him dry. All the while the calf's eyes were closed, and whether he ever blinked I can't say. But he was not showing any possible sign of wanting to live, and he was as stiff as a frozen wet blanket would have been hanging on a clothesline outdoors in that sub-freezing temperature. His tongue was several inches out of his mouth, and he obviously could not swallow or roll his eyes about. I thought I saw weak breathing, so I continued my efforts.

I went in for my electric heating pad and placed that on his mid-section and plugged it in. I remembered that my closest neighbor had raised chicks and used several heat lamps, so I took the pickup and drove over there to see about borrowing one. She had one to spare.

I hung the heat lamp in place over where I perceived his heart and lungs to be located, and I went into the house for a half-hour. I found some first milk in the freezer, saved from another cow. Milk taken from a cow immediately after giving birth contains colostrum, and it is necessary for a calf to drink this shortly after birth. I began thawing it by setting it in a pan of hot water.

I went to check on the calf. His mid-section still felt cold despite the heating pad and heat lamp, and his head and limbs were still as cold to my touch as a chunk of meat from the freezer. I knew instinctively that he needed massage to awaken the circulation, or he was a loser.

I looked at my watch as I began rubbing his legs, and it was about 10 o'clock. A half hour later I had rubbed all of his limbs vigorously, and my own arthritic knees and weak back were groaning under the strain. I moved closer to his head and sat down in the straw and began to rub his jaws and throat and to slap his cheeks. He tried to retract his tongue a little and began to shiver ever so slightly. I continued massage with renewed hope. Another half hour went by, and he was now really shivering. I had to rest, so I put the heat lamp over him again and went into the house to lie down for a half hour.

The calf I found at noon was struggling to live. His eyeballs were rolling around, and he was trying to retract his tongue. His shivering had not diminished, but that meant simply that his circulation was continuing to improve. I worked at giving more massage. Then I decided to try feeding some of that milk. I went in and warmed about two cups of milk and put it into a plastic bag with an attached feeding tube. I stuck the end of the tube into his mouth, but the milk just ran onto the floor. He was still unable to swallow. So I really gave his head and throat a vigorous massage and then propped up his head and shoulders with a bale of hay. He slid back onto the straw repeatedly, but each effort improved his circulation. Some time later when he was able to hold his wobbly head in an upright position, I arranged his legs under him so that he could lie there like a proper calf.

My back and sore knees were screaming in protest by now, so I went in to take a double dose of pain killer. I knew that I had saved him if I could get him to drink. I warmed another batch of milk and headed for the barn.

This time I straddled him and put the feeding tube into his mouth. He was still unable to swallow properly, but some of the milk found the way down as he coughed and struggled. I decided to pull him upward into a standing position. He was like a heavy lump of concrete with spaghetti legs, but after several attempts he was able to stand while I straddled him. Then I tried the milk again, and some of it got into him.

Throughout the entire day the mother cow had been in the adjacent pen, sometimes eating hay, sometimes lowing to her calf. I wondered if she understood I was trying to help him.

By now the calf was able to stand alone on wobbly legs, so I thought it was time to let the mother in to him. I opened her gate. She came to the calf at once, sniffed him, and walked away. I feared there was none of his scent left on him, only mine. But she turned and came back for another sniff, walking away again. Eventually she lingered and took a lick at him with her tongue. The calf responded by nuzzling her belly. She stood still, and in no time at all he found his mother's teats and began sucking.

I watched them awhile to make sure all was going well, and then I picked up my paraphernalia and went into the house. There I was faced with a pile of soiled kettles in which I had warmed milk and with dirty breakfast dishes. It was time to get supper. I grabbed a slice of bread as I had not eaten anything since an early breakfast. I took more pain pills. We would have to settle for soup and sandwiches tonight as I simply had to lie down awhile.

I was up again at 6:30 p.m.when my husband drove into the yard. He parked the car beside the barn and went through the south doorway, no doubt to pull out the dead calf. He said, when he came into the house, that he could not believe his eyes when he was met by a big, romping, lively calf!

I named the calf Lazarus. I had not raised him from the dead, but he had been very nearly dead. I had prayed hard for God's help while I struggled, and I had been given a minor miracle.

Lazarus thrived and was soon outdoors with his mother. For many days he would come running to me when I approached the pen. He thought I was his mother!

A lady friend from the city said to me, when she heard of the effort, "Well, you know you have to try to save every calf with the price of beef being what it is."

"The price of beef! I wasn't thinking of the price of beef," I said. Well, she simply did not understand. Here was a perfectly formed, beautiful animal, dying unless cared for. He needed my help. I simply had to save him if I could. He deserved better than to die of hypothermia, and the mother cow deserved her calf. It was simply the right thing to do.

The Waterhole Episode

Every spring morning on our farm John would head out to the barn to check on any possible calving cows before eating breakfast. He kept the heifers there during calving, but the older cows who had calved before were in the south forty. If calving seemed imminent, he made trips to the barn at night until a cow had successfully calved.

This particular April morning was his 73rd birthday. Something told him to go to the pasture first.

He started up his Diesel tractor with a cab on it and headed for the older cows. As he approached the first square waterhole, he saw something very white in the water. What could that be? There were no stones in the water, he thought. Cows were lying resting within a few feet of the water's edge. One cow was pacing and mooing beside the deep end. Then he realized that the white blob was the head of a calf. Dead, no doubt, he thought.

Getting closer, he saw that the calf was alive and swimming, trying to stay close to its mother. The afterbirth lay by the water's edge, so it was evident the calf had slid into the water at birth because his mother had lain down too close to the water's edge. Either that or he had lost his balance on one of his first efforts at trying out his wobbly legs and had fallen in.

What to do now, John wondered. John cannot swim, and he had brought no equipment along for this kind of rescue. It was barely above freezing and had been colder during the night. Anyhow, the water had to be dreadfully cold. He did not know how long the calf had been in the water.

John walked over to a fence line and cut out a 6-foot chunk of barbed wire with the pliers he kept in his pocket. He fashioned a loop and knelt to try to catch the calf's head. But the head slipped out of the loop each time he tried pulling the calf to the edge. Then he went from the end of the waterhole to one side, thus getting the calf's head from a different angle. After several attempts he had the calf pulled to the edge and was able to grab it by one leg and pulled it to dry land. He dragged the cold, shivering calf several feet away from the water.

He left it alone there, and the mother came to claim and wash her calf. John drove home and checked on his other heifers, thinking the calf might die of extreme exposure before he could get back to try to help.

"Come and help!" he yelled at me through the kitchen door about twenty minutes later. "I found a newborn calf in the waterhole, but I got him out," he said. "I want you to help me get him home."

"What about the cow?" I asked.

"We'll take her home, too, of course," he answered.

I did not need to ask how we would get them home. It was

not the first time I helped with this kind of problem. I put on warmer clothes and a navy jacket with a snorkle hood. The pasture lay high in the penetrating April wind, and it was still early in the day.

I prepared a needle and syringe for a penicillin shot. John hooked the tractor onto the hayrack this time, so I rode on the rack.

The Waterhole Calf

The calf lay where John had left him and seemed unable to get up. But John gave him the shot, anyway. The sudden jab of the needle got life into him, and he sprang to his feet. He wasn't as bad off as we had thought, unless he was already getting pneumonia.

John and I struggled to lift the heavy bull calf onto the hayrack. His mamma mooed and sniffed and kept her eye on him. I straddled the calf and sat on him, holding him in place on the hayrack as John drove slowly homeward. The cow followed closely.

John put the calf right inside the open barn door, and the cow who had followed protectingly all the way to the barn now entered, and John shut the door.

After a week of special care and more shots, the calf seemed totally well and frisky. Mother and son went out to pasture again.

The Waterhole Calf grew into a handsome bull and is, at last report, someone's happy herd bull.

Strange and Special Cats I Have Known

I read once that Russian blue cats are thought to be the best hunters among domestic cats. One of my favorite childhood cats was a Russian blue female, the most terrific hunter among the cats I have known.

She was not remarkable to look at, just a solid slate-gray cat with no other markings. She might even have been considered ugly by comparison with striped and calico cats. Her outstanding hunting and survival abilities more than made up for her plain appearance. We first called her Mamma Cat because she was the mother to most of the cats on our farm, but soon she was dubbed Grandma Cat because she was the senior cat among generations of cats and kittens, not only on our farm but in our neighborhood. She outlived all the others.

My little flock of white Pekin ducklings had been noisily begging for food one morning when I was about twelve years old, and I went to the granary to get some middlings for making wet mash. The middlings (coarse particles of ground wheat mixed with bran) were in a huge sack on the floor in a corner of the old wood granary. Grandma Cat followed me in my activities, and as I struggled with the heavy sack, her nose told her what was under it. The instant I slid the sack a foot across the floor, she went into action, pouncing on a mouse nest which was under the sack. I barely had time to glimpse the pinkish, half-grown baby mice before she had squirming mice under each paw and two in her mouth. She hesitated less than a second, then proceeded to crunch the ones in her mouth, dropping them dead on the floor, then killing the ones under her one front paw, then the other, and at last the singles under each back paw. She looked up at me for praise, and I counted seven dead mice, including the mother mouse. Seven in less than 15 seconds.

Grandma Cat kept mice and rats from destroying bushels of valuable grain on our farm for sixteen years. She caught dozens and dozens of gophers as well, and at least one woodchuck. She had two batches of kittens every summer, and it must have contributed to her good health because she was never ill. She survived the hooves of cows and horses in the barn, the wheels and sickle blades of farm machinery in motion, and rabies and distemper and all manner of disease for which she was never given a preventative shot. She survived blizzards, hail, and tornados when she was out hunting and found herself far from the yard or locked out of the barn when she got home. Grandma Cat was a champion!

One of Grandma Cat's kittens, a chubby, gray-striped kitten with a white belly and white front toes, grew into a husky, powerful, big-boned cat, beautiful and good-natured. I named him Lars. He enjoyed petting and purred lustily to show appreciation while smiling as only a content cat can.

Lars loved sweet treats and crunched-up hard ribbon candy when he was given a small piece each Christmas. I taught him to perform for various treats by walking upright on his hind legs. Of course he rested his forepaws on my hand while he did this, but he could carry on in this unnatural manner for a full minute and seemed to enjoy it.

Imagine my surprise and amazement when Lars, at the age of three, gave birth to four kittens out on the yard one summer day! "He" dropped them, one here and one there, and turned to devour each of them in turn. Lars never had kittens again in the three or four more years that he lived. I was twelve years old at the time and could tell adult female cats from adult males, so I simply do not have an explanation, nor did my parents ever come to an understanding of how this had happened. Even after his brief "motherhood" we continued to call "him" Lars.

When my husband, daughter and I moved to our Glenwood farm in 1973, we brought along our housecat from Wahpeton, a long-haired calico named Tiger whom everyone had begun calling "Tuddyhoppin'." (Don't ask.) For the first five years of Tuddyhoppin's life she had been let outdoors only when on a harness and leash. She had a very difficult time adjusting to her freedom on the farm. She feared and fought every other cat and small animal she encountered, and her long fur was constantly full of weed seeds and burs. She also feared the horses, the cows, the dog and the sound of thunder.

Tuddyhoppin' had two distinct "pussonality" traits. She was as cantankerous at times as she was sociable on other occasions. You could pet her for about two minutes in the mornings, but from then on she'd give you her best punch. And speaking of punch, she was left-handed. Or left-pawed. No doubt about it. Every time she batted at something, she always used her left paw. Most cats seem to be ambidextrous, but this cat used her right front paw only for walking or climbing.

Mindy, Age 6o, as Farmer's Wife

Photo by Karen Willmus

Despite her independence and cantankerousness, she loved being around people. She was social and playful to the point of being dangerous to humans, biting and scratching in her enthusiastic playfulness. If any cat should have been declawed, it was Tuddyhoppin'.

One warm summer evening just after dark we heard a hair-raising growl that only a cat cornered by an adversary or a cat in great pain could make. My husband hurried out the door to find a wide-eyed, soaking-wet Tuddyhoppin' crouching in the corner by the garage door. She sent him threats and would have nothing to do with him, so he came in and ordered me out to deal with her. She had considerably more confidence in me, albeit very little at that point, but I managed to pick her up and transport the protesting, struggling body into the basement where I shut her in a small room. There she spent the rest of the night growling in real or imagined pain.

By morning Tuddyhoppin' was calm enough for an examination. Her left front leg had a vicious-looking but bloodless bruise that looked as though something had pinched her severely. This, and the fact that she was soaking wet when we found her, got me to wondering what in the world had happened to her. It became less of a mystery when I remembered that I had seen her hunting along the edge of the slough beside our driveway that afternoon. I believe Tuddyhoppin' had batted at a huge snapping turtle with her left paw and had been grabbed by that turtle and pulled into the water. I can only imagine the struggle she had and how she got free from him before he would manage to drown her!

Our farm has the driveway built through a shallow slough from the main road up to the yard. When we moved there, we gained a beautiful calico female cat whom we named Mamma Kitty because she was the mamma to all the other cats on the farm and several neighbor cats. She loved to hunt and caught rats, pocket gophers and striped gophers, and innumerable mice. She, like Tuddyhoppin', often hunted along the edge of the driveway. Her specialty, however, was to hunt bullheads from the slough. She would sit crouched at the edge of the murky water and stare into it until she spotted an unsuspecting bullhead swimming up close. In one wet pounce Mamma Kitty would hook the bullhead, and she'd dine on it right there in the grassy edge. What she didn't eat, a great blue heron finished.

Tomas, Norwegian for Thomas, was a reckless, daring fellow who was handsome as well, a gray tabby with a white belly and white collar. He was also about eighty percent clown. He loved high places and was especially attracted to the hay carrier track in our Gothic-roofed barn. That was because a colony of pigeons roosted on that high track.

As I climbed into the hay mow for a bale of hay one day, I spotted Tomas lying on the track way up underneath the cupula, and he had one foreleg on either side of the track with his claws embedded in a struggling pigeon below. He couldn't move without letting go of the pigeon, which he was loath to do. He obviously could not make up his "furry" mind whether to lose the pigeon and come down, or keep the pigeon and sit up there all day. After I called to him by name a few times, he lost his concentration altogether, and the pigeon flew away.

One sunny spring day, Tomas was outside–on top of the barn roof, in fact! That high, round roof still had wood shingles. Old, rotting ones. He was way out on the peak that covers the start of the hay track, and he lay there with both forelegs over the edge, batting at a pigeon perched under the overhang.

Tomas clung to the roof with the claws of his hind feet, but then, in his determination to get the pigeon, he put his outer hind leg over the edge, too, with only the claws of one hind foot embedded in the disintegrating shingles! I nearly had a heart attack. I yelled at him to get down. Then I remembered I must CALL a cat, not issue orders. "Tomas! Tomas! Come, Tomas!" I almost screamed. "Tomas! Come, Tomas!"

He skillfully backed up onto the roof with all four paws, turned, and was down on the ground in seconds.

"Meow," he said as he looked up at me as if to ask, "What did you want, Ma?"

Tomas preferred to stay in our garage on rainy days. On one such day I was at work in the kitchen adjacent to the garage, when I heard something metallic bang loudly onto the cement floor of the garage. I dropped my work and stepped through the doorway onto the landing. I noted the aluminum ladder lying diagonally across the floor as Tomas came dragging his rather limp body up the three steps of the landing. He fell at my feet as he let out an awful respiratory noise much like the noise an inflated balloon makes when one lets it go and it loses air rapidly. I wondered if Tomas was going to die at my feet. He let out another desperate rattle, and I stooped to press on his rib cage as he seemed not to be able to breathe. Then these noises began to come in quicker succession.

I took him up into my arms, went inside and laid him on a soft rug in a corner of the kitchen. There he rested and continued his diminishing noises in regular rhythm for at least an hour. At last he went to sleep, and even in sleep I could hear little sobs of pain. I knew by then that he simply could not resist climbing the tall ladder which had been propped up against the wall. It had been too upright for his considerable weight, so it tipped and fell backward with Tomas clutching it, falling across his ribs and knocking the air out of his lungs.

Tomas never did learn to be cautious. He continued to live dangerously, and he did not always stay around home, neutered though he was. He was struck by a car one dark night as he darted onto the highway in characteristic haste. He was thrown thirty feet, stone dead. Life had been a big, daring adventure, short and sweet.

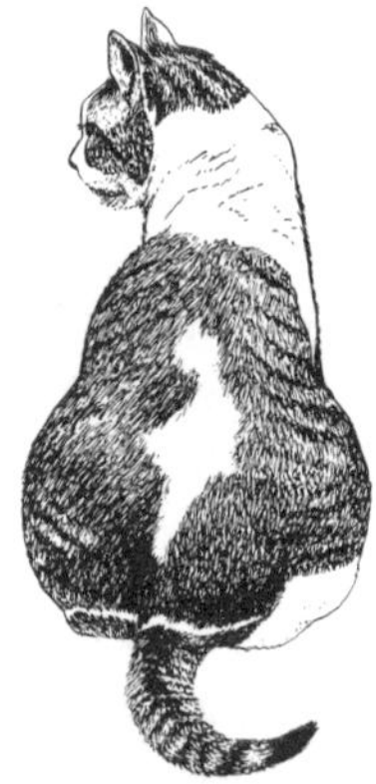

Lars II

On a June night Lars II was born in our Glenwood farm garage. He was a very large, hang-loose kind of kitten who grew into a very heavy-duty cat of around sixteen pounds. He would have gained more weight had he been housebound, but he was free to hunt six months out of the year. The rest of the year he spent in the house where he had better manners than most kids I have known.

Lars was a beautiful, grey-striped tabby with white underparts and feet, a white collar around the neck, and a finer white ring around the base of the tail. His face had a white, totally symmetrical curtain-shaped area between the eyes, leaving his nose and cheeks white as well. A distinct black line ran from the corner of his eyes back around his temples, looking like a fine makeup job. He had similar black vertical stripes from his eyes up his forehead. But the most comical marking was a quarter-size black spot on each hind leg at exactly the same height. Down his back was an artistic, random zigzag of white. God could not have planned a more perfect pattern for a cat.

Large cats like Lars find ingenious ways to hunt as well as ways to avoid much walking in the process. His favorite method of hunting was to climb a railroad-tie corner post in the fence, settle in comfortably on top, and then stare patiently down into the grass below. When an unsuspecting mouse or vole came along, he would spring off the post in sure and silent flight like a hawk. He rarely failed at this tactic and demonstrated that patience and tenacity are great virtues.

Lars was good natured and friendly, never obnoxious in getting attention. He made people remember him by his friendliness, and several times he got greetings by way of letters to me from cat lovers.

Lars, like most male cats, had a weak, high-pitched voice. He seldom used his voice. He answered my calls if he heard my voice and came promptly when out of doors. Otherwise I heard his voice only if I accidentally stepped on his tail.

Lars was a housecat by night and during the winter. He never abused the privilege by clawing my furniture, my drapes, or the carpets. Nor was he declawed. Some few cats seem to know how to live like "aristocats." He even enjoyed nature programs on TV, seating himself on the floor about four feet in front of the set. If there was a lot of animal or bird action, he often watched the whole of Marty Stoufer films with undivided attention, relaxing only during commercials.

One big adventure he never managed to tell me about occurred when he was three years old. He was neutered when very young, and he came home from his short hunting trips every day. But this spring day he did not return. I called for him, but I thought he would surely be home by morning. He was not there the next morning, either. I walked through the neighboring woods and over all the fields and called for him. He had always been faithful to answer my call and to come. He just was not there. I repeated this search twice a day through rain and shine every day. I called at the top of my lungs so that people and critters surely heard me a half-mile or more from where I walked. I also telephoned neighbors, and no one had seen him. I prayed for his safety all the while, not bearing to think of him suffering at the hands of cruel people.

On the 18th day of his absence, as I was baking cookies, I looked up and out the window to see Lars hurrying across the yard toward the house! What joy to see him! I ran to open the door, and he came in without as much as a greeting and went straight for his favorite chair and settled in. I petted and hugged him, but he wanted to be left alone.

Four hours later he awakened and went to his litter box. Next stop, the refrigerator. There he seated himself and looked up at the door handle. I got the message, and he soon had milk, water and food. He slept all night in the rocking chair.

The next morning I weighed him, and he was at least two pounds lighter than before, and his foot pads were all criss-crossed with small cuts and were bruised and dirty.

Each morning he awoke, shook his grates, ate, and went back to sleep. This he repeated in late afternoon. Five days went by before he asked to go outdoors. Lars never left home again. I believe someone stole him, for he was friendly and unafraid, and took him quite far from home. Cats with a strong bond to someone at home do not get lost.

Lars II lived a good, useful life, giving pleasure to me and many others for fifteen years. He took his secrets with him, telling no one.

Swinger was a basic black cat with a generous amount of gold hair in her fur, scattered like stardust. All four black feet had white toes making them look like they had on spats such as men wore over their shoes in the '20's. She was a great hunter and ate a lot of chipmunks, but chipmunks are very easy to catch. It was downright difficult to be a cat and NOT catch chipmunks in our yard as there were so many of them that a cat almost stumbled over them.

I came out from our garage one afternoon to see Swinger playing with a live chipmunk. The critter had rolled itself into a ball, playing dead, and Swinger was tossing it into the air with her right hook to the fur. When the cat saw me, she came toward me, abandoning the uninjured chipmunk. I retreated into the garage, closing the door. I saw through the door window that Swinger went back to where she had left the chipmunk and lay down, flat on her belly. Meanwhile, the chipmunk had disappeared, and Swinger was midway between the house and our huge bur oak tree.

In a few minutes I had another errand out doors, and as I walked out from the garage, the chipmunk came out from under my spirea bush by the house wall and fled in terror from my human presence to the safest place in the shortest distance–under the belly of the cat! Right in front of Swinger's folded hind legs the chipmunk hid!

As I walked in their direction, Swinger got up and began a leisurely walk toward the oak tree. The befuddled chipmunk lingered momentarily before fear of my human form spurred him into action. He ran the shortest distance to the oak tree which meant that he had to catch up with the cat and pass her, running broadside with her momentarily before gaining speed to be the first to climb the oak tree. No need to fear. The cat was bored with him and simply let him pass by. I wondered, are they friends or enemies?

My last cat was a fifteen-year-old calico female whom my daughter had named Kit 'n Kaboodle. Boodle for short. And short she was. She reminded me of a wiry little old lady, a nag and a gossip. Boodle loved to talk. She was the most communi"cat"ive animal I've known, always commenting on something or making a request. My husband hated her for nagging.

She also had a large people-vocabulary. She knew many words and reacted to them with understanding. For example, while Boodle lay curled into a ball on my lap in front of the TV with her eyes covered by her paws, if I should say anything at all using the words, "go to bed," she would spring from my lap and tear into the bedroom to hide under my bed because she did not like to "go to bed" in her basement room. Under my bed is where she hid when guests came, too.

Kaboodle's colors were fine for a calico, with evenly distributed white, orange, and black areas, but her orange had a faint suggestion of stripe in it. Pretty good for a barn-bred cat, though. Her foot pads were all black as a true calico's should be. Kaboodle's fur was longer than that of most cats, but she was a short-hair. What is remarkable is that her fur was silky and soft as down.

Kaboodle hunted outdoors in summer, and mice were her specialty. She would come to the landing by the front door, announcing her catch. She actually smiled when I praised her. Then, with my blessing, she dined on her mouse, leaving only a tiny heap of entrails. A neat butcher.

No cat was ever a better house cat than Kaboodle. She clawed only the one carpet she had permission to claw, and she often spent whole days at home alone without injury to anything. Her "pussonality," her softness, and her cuteness (short legs, smallness, and vivid colors) as well as her complete confidence in me all added up to keeping my blood pressure low and keeping faith that there is goodness in all of God's creatures here in this harsh world.

Kaboodle, the Gentle Calico Lady

The Way I See It

Mother and Father lived long, and theirs was an age of tremendous material progress. Both were born before the advent of the first successful gasoline-powered automobile and before the invention of the airplane. Yet, both lived to see Neil Armstrong walk on the moon–on their new black and white television screen!

In the medical field they witnessed the virtual end of tuberculosis in our nation, the coming of vaccinations of several kinds, the coming of aspirin, penicillin and other antibiotics, and of spinal fusions, organ transplants, and scanners.

As farmers they went from horses for power to tractors, from gasoline engines to electric motors, and from kerosene lamps to electric lights. The pot-bellied coal heater gave way to an oil furnace, and the wood kitchen range was no longer needed for heat and was replaced by gas and electric ranges. Mother's pantry was given up in favor of a refrigerator and a deep freeze. They saw mowers, hayrakes, and grain binders give way to haybines and combines.

My father's neighbors called him "Flying Ekeberg" for a time because he drove his first car, a Model T Ford, all of 17 miles per hour. His last car was an American Motors 1968 Rambler and could easily exceed the 70 mile per hour speed limit on the interstate highway.

Much of all this also happened during my lifetime. In addition, we have the luxuries of colored television and cable TV, a video cassette recorder and a camcorder, a microwave oven, and a new, spacious van. The computer and the fax machine are now commonplace.

Human creativity in this period also led to devastating consequences. We invented the atomic bomb and engaged in the Holocaust. More recently there is widespread improper use of drugs, of the gun, of sex, and even of that marvelous invention, the camera!

Many exciting things are happening in research in medicine, genetics, and studies of the human body. But just as tuberculosis and infantile paralysis remained unconquered when I was a little girl, we still have no cure for cancer. And now we have AIDS.

We are just recently learning how to care for our

environment and discovering some of the results of our destruction of our forests and various habitats. Individuals and industry are becoming more accountable regarding the environment. There is hope.

The family farm as a way of life is still hanging on for an ever-decreasing number of people. There will always be farms in some form, I think, and families will live on them and be the workers and caretakers. There is hope.

Most people still believe in the merits of home and family even though the character of the family now has many forms and definitions. Much discussion and research is going on here, too. There is hope.

Just as one neighbor assisted another in times of trouble in the 1930's, we are beginning to see city dwellers becoming more personally involved working with their neighbors in making their communities safer and more attractive. Some of these efforts have been highly successful. There is hope.

At times I get discouraged and think we are standing still or even regressing regarding human rights. Then I remember when I was going to college in 1952, I chose to take the only remaining seat on a Greyhound bus–after the driver, standing at the front of the bus, announced that the bus was filled. The seat was among eight or ten black women and two black men in the rear of the bus. There is hope.

We seem to be losing our faith and our values. The hope I see here lies in the observation that human history is like a pendulum. There are "swings" from one extreme viewpoint and lifestyle to another. Each generation has its own peculiar problems, failures, and successes. It might be good to take a thoughtful look at life in the 1930's to discover what values we would wish to regain.

What challenges will the next generation meet? What will they accomplish for the benefit of humanity? As long as we continue to search for truth and knowledge and an understanding of ourselves and our world, there is hope.

Acknowledgements

My sincere appreciaton and thanks go to my husband who gave me bits of advice and had faith in me, and to my daughter who gave me much advice and assistance as well as support when I felt doubts about this project.

Thanks go to the several persons who encouraged me to put these narratives into book form, to Frank Schmainda for very valuable editorial assistance, and to those who read my script and wrote endorsements. I also extend thanks to the patient, helpful staff at Echo Printing. Others helped in many small ways, and to them I am also grateful.

Mildred Gaasland

ORDER FORM

Send ______ copies of Mindy at $9.95 each $_____.___

Plus 6.5% sales tax ($.65 per copy)
Minnesota residents only _____.___

Plus $1.50 for one copy packaging and
postage, additional copies .25 each _____.___

Total enclosed $_____.___

Mail to:
Name ____________________

Address ____________________

City, State, Zip ____________________

Mail order and payment to:
Pekin Publications
523 Second Ave. N.E.
Glenwood, MN 56334-1407

Checks are to be made out to Pekin Publications. No books shipped without prepayment.